Prayer After the Slaughter
The Great War: Poems and Stories from World War I
Kurt Tucholsky

Prayer After The Slaughter

The Great War: Poems and Stories from Wold War I

Kurt Tucholsky

Translated by Peter Appelbaum and James Scott

New York, 2015

Prayer After the Slaughter
By Kurt Tucholsky

Translators: Peter Appelbaum, James Scott
Editor: Eva C. Schweitzer
Copy editor: Mark LaFlaur

© 2015 by Berlinica Publishing LLC
255 West 43rd St., Suite 1012
New York, NY, 10036, USA

Print book ISBN:
978-3-96026-020-2
Ebook ISBN:
978-1-935902-24-9
978-1-935902-29-4
978-1-935902-32-4
LCCN: 2014956233

Photos: Kurt Tucholsky Gesellschaft p. 6
Public Domain: pp: 28, 36, 62, 76, 96
Cover photo: John Henry Dolph, Playing Cat and Mouse

Kurt Tucholsky Society: www.tucholsky-gesellschaft.de
Tucholsky Museum: http://www.tucholsky-museum.de

Printed in the United States
All rights reserved under International and Pan-American Copyright Law. No part of this book may be used or reproduced in any manner whatsoever without written permission except in the case of brief quotations embodied in critical articles and reviews.

www.berlinica.com, blog.berlinica.com

*Let us agree that, when we speak of these years, we call it:
The Great Time.*

Kurt Tucholsky

Kurt Tucholsky in 1915, in his Word War I uniform. The poet, writer, and journalist came back from the war experience deeply traumatized and a lifelong pacifist.
Picture: Kurt Tucholsky Society

Contents

Preface by Noah Isenberg	9
Die Katze spielt mit der Maus /	14–15
The Cat Plays With The Mouse	
Memento / Memento	20–21
Das Grammophon / The Gramophone	22–23
Der Kriegslieferant / The War Contractor	30–31
Zum Ersten August / August First	32–33
Kolonne / The Convoy	34–35
Helm ab –! / Helmet Off–!	38–39
Weihnachten / Christmas	40–41
Zwei Erschlagene / Two Clubbed to Death	42–43
Militaria: Unser Militär / 'Our Military'	46–47
Kriegsgefangen / Prisoner of War	60–61
Krieg dem Kriege / Make War on War	64–65
Na, mein Sohn? / Well, My Son?	68–69
S'ist Krieg / It's War	72–73
Nach fünf Jahren / Five Years Later	74–75
Zwei Mann: Gitarre und Mandoline /	78–79
Two Men: Guitar and Mandolin	
Der Krieg ohne Namen /	82–83
The War Without Name	
Das erdolchte Heer / The Backstabbed Army	86–87
Ich habe noch . . . / I still have . . .	88–89
Der Mantel / The Coat	98–99
Die Flecke / White Spots	102–103
Gebet nach dem Schlachten /	106–107
Prayer After The Slaughter	

Biographies

PETER APPELBAUM MD, PH.D., is Emeritus Professor of Pathology, Pennsylvania State University. His interests in German and modern Jewish history led to his discovery of the lives of the 100,000 Jewish soldiers in the WWI German army. He wrote two books. *Loyalty Betrayed: Jewish Chaplains in the German Army During the First World War* and *Loyal Sons. German Jews in the First World War.* He also has unearthed and translated poetry written by German Jewish soldiers.

JAMES W. SCOTT, PH.D., is Emeritus Professor of German at Lebanon Valley College in Annville, PA. His scholarly presentations have ranged from Rainer Maria Rilke's prose and Franz Kafka's short fiction to cabaret in East Germany. He is editing Ebernand von Erfurt's *Kaiser und Kaiserin* and is preparing a new translation of *Iwein,* by Hartmann von Aue.

CINDY OPITZ is a translator and art historian from Iowa. She has translated numerous works by Kurt Tucholsky, including *Berlin! Berlin! Dispatches From the Weimar Republic.*

NOAH ISENBERG is Professor and Chair of the Department of Culture and Media at The New School for Liberal Arts, in New York City, and the author of Edgar G. Ulmer: *A Filmmaker at the Margins.* Among his other books is *Between Redemption and Doom: The Strains of German-Jewish Modernism.*

Rediscovering Kurt Tucholsky

By Noah Isenberg

KURT TUCHOLSKY was a literary star in his day, and indeed he continues to retain some of that initial luster throughout German-speaking Europe. The Berlin-born and bred writer—who entered the world in the largely working-class district of Moabit on January 9, 1890, the eldest son of a well-to-do, assimilated, German-Jewish family—became best known during the tumultuous years of the Weimar Republic, contributing regularly to such prominent publications as the left-leaning weekly *Die Weltbühne* (The World Stage), which he also edited for a short stretch in the mid-1920s. During this period he wrote mainly political and cultural criticism; under such memorable, evocative pseudonyms as Ignaz Wrobel, Theobald Tiger, Peter Panter and Kaspar Hauser, used in part to dispel the notion that most articles in the *Weltbühne* came from the same author. They were salvos in an oft-satirical spirit aimed at the crusty, backwards-glancing conservatives, at the deep and imposing vestiges of Prussian bureaucracy, and at the rising wave of militarism and National Socialist fervor.

No single event, however, affected Tucholsky more than World War I. His staunch anti-militarism spawning the series of texts, both literary essays and lyrical poetry, collected in *Prayer After the Slaughter*, a remarkable book that gives English-speaking readers the chance to discover one of the most gifted writers of the so-called Generation of 1914 on

the centennial anniversary of World War I, also known as the Great War.

Tucholsky was drafted—like so many other young Germans and German Jews, yet without the patriotic fervor shared especially among students and intellectuals—into the Imperial army in April 1915. There he eventually served, just as his friend, the writer Arnold Zweig had done in Lithuania, in the military press division at Alt-Autz, in what is today Latvia, editing the newspaper *Der Flieger* (The Pilot). Still later, by then stationed in Romania, he did a stint in the military police, where he must have gathered ample material for his future skewering of German officialdom. The experience made him a lifelong pacifist.

After he returned to Germany, when the war had ended, Tucholsky wrote with feverish intensity, contributing more than 1,800 pieces, poetry and prose, to the *Weltbühne*—the kind of prodigious output rivaled perhaps only by his Viennese counterpart, Karl Kraus, that other acid-tongued critic who took similar pleasure in his high-octane literary take-downs and slinging of barbed prose aimed squarely and unflinchingly at the establishment. Tucholsky also wrote cabaret lyrics, and published a number of separate books: in 1919. As Theobald Tiger, he released a volume of poetry *Fromme Gesänge* (Pious Cantos); in 1920, the same year that he wrote lyrics for the anti-militarist chanson "Rote Melodie" ("Red Melody"), he published a collection of "bourgeois fairytales" *Träumereien an preussischen Kaminen* (Reveries by Prussian Firesides), released as Peter Panter. In 1927, he wrote *Ein Pyrenäenbuch* (A Book of the Pyrenees), a travelogue from his visit to the region two years earlier. In collaboration with the Dada artist John Heartfield, he published his provocatively titled *Deutschland, Deutschland über alles*, a biting critique of the political culture of his day (lambasting such figures

as Adolf Hitler and Hermann Göring), in 1929. Soon after, Tucholsky abandoned Germany for Sweden, where he wrote his novel *Schloss Gripsholm* (Gripsholm Castle). It was a runaway bestseller, taking him back to some extent to the core themes, to the romance and the levity, of *Rheinsberg—ein Bilderbuch für Verliebte* (Rheinsberg: A Storybook for Lovers), his first major literary success (also published in English translation by Berlinica).

He was married twice, first and rather briefly to Else Weil, a medical doctor in Weimar Berlin, who is widely credited with having inspired the character of Claire in *Rheinsberg*. Later, he married a woman he met during his military service, the Riga-born Mary Gerold. Mary's farewell letter, given to him after their split, he purportedly carried with him in his breast pocket until the day he died of a drug overdose, on December 21, 1935, in a Gothenburg hospital near his house in Hindås, Sweden. Just a few weeks after his death, on this side of the Atlantic, *The New York Times* ran an obituary with the following words: "More than any other person, he foresaw what was coming there, and that was one of the reasons why after the Nazi revolution he virtually never wrote anything on the subject ... What his readers had enjoyed as the capricious fantasies of a clever satirist has now been enacted with bitter reality." After the Nazis rose to power, Tucholsky enjoyed the dubious distinction of having his books among the first to be burned in May 1933.

To read Tucholsky's war poetry and prose today is to experience the profound sense of righteous indignation, even betrayal, that very few German authors had the courage to articulate; let alone the sobriety to recognize the moral turpitude in what was then frequently passed off as benign patriotism. Take, for example, "Memento," published pseudonymously as Theobald Tiger in November 1916 in *Die*

Schaubühne (the precursor to *Die Weltbühne*), which assails the power elite for leading the young recruits to slaughter: "Tell your youth of all the warrior's virtues / But tell him, too, amid the clashing steel / that all his youthful dreams as well / must have their due, if he would be a man!" The cruel ironies that belie the great promise of "national rebirth" come further into view in the period photo, of euphoric German soldiers heading off to the Western Front in 1914, included in the Berlinica edition.

In his prose piece "Militaria: 'Our Military,'" Tucholsky, then writing as Ignaz Wrobel in *Die Weltbühne* in February 1920, pulls no punches when he concludes, "We spit on the military." It is unsurprising that his poem "It's War," equally ferocious in its assault on the profiteers and battle strategists, was banned during the war. "For what did we give the red blood of our hearts away?" asks the title poem, followed by the poignant, unforgiving lines: "The Kaiser has six and they're all still living today. / There was a time we believed . . . Oh how stupid we were . . . ! / They made us all drunk . . . / Why?"

When I was a graduate student in German studies at Berkeley in the early 1990s, and was searching for an appropriate dissertation topic, I remember becoming increasingly interested in this seemingly obscure literary figure known as Tucholsky, who despite having been translated into some fourteen other languages had not found much of an Anglo-American critical reception. I was drawn especially to his wit and his courage, to his unremitting energy and his extraordinary sensitivity to language. In the end, I didn't write a thesis on Tucholsky, but the writers I chose to address instead all had deep ties to him: Kafka had met with him during an early visit to Prague; Arnold Zweig enjoyed a passionate and unusually candid correspondence with Tucholsky in his later years (they both recognized,

with bracing honesty, the grave predicament in which German Jews of their generation had found themselves); and Walter Benjamin shared with Tucholsky not only a penchant for edgy, spirited criticism, but would also later find himself a "discontinued German" (as Tucholsky said of himself in 1932, as if his shelf life had simply run out). Some eight decades later, the timeliness of Tucholsky's writing has not waned a bit, and thanks to the efforts of Berlinica, English-speaking readers finally have access to some of his finest work.

Kurt Tucholsky

Die Katze spielt mit der Maus

Peter Panter, *Die Schaubühne,*
9. November 1916

Sie stehen alle im Kreis, die Soldaten, und blicken alle auf einen Punkt. Ich trete hinzu.

Die schwarz-weiße Katze hat eine Maus gefangen. Die schwarz-weiße Katze, unser Kompanie-Peter (eine Dame, allerdings), Peter der Erste; ein junges Tier, noch nicht völlig ausgewachsen, aber auch nicht mehr niedlich genug, um in die Hand genommen zu werden. Die Maus ist noch springlebendig – Peter muß sie eben erst gefangen haben. Peter ist tagelang auf dem Kriegsschauplatz herumgelaufen, Peter hat sich eigenmächtig von der Truppe entfernt, also hat sie Hunger, also wird sie die Maus gleich fressen.

Die Katze läßt die Maus laufen. Die Maus flitzt, wie an einer Schnur gezogen, davon – die Katze mit einem genau abgeschätzten Sprung nach. Mit der letzten Spitze der ausgestreckten Pfote hält sie die Maus. Die Maus zappelt. Die Pfote schiebt sich langsam hin und her; die Pfote prüft die Maus. Die Katze liegt dahinter und dirigiert das Ganze. Aber das ist nicht mehr ihre Pfote – das ist ein neues Tier, das nur für den Zweck erschaffen ist, ein wenig, so grausam wenig schneller als die Maus zu sein. Die Pfote hebt sich, die Maus stürzt davon – sie darf stürzen, ja, das ist gradezu vorgesehen. Die Pfote waltet ihr zu Häupten und schlägt sie im letzten Augenblick nieder. Die Maus quiekt. Jetzt wird das Tempo lebhafter.

Hurr – die Maus läuft, ein weites Stück. Satz. Hat. Und wieder – und wieder. Manchmal sieht die Katze mit ihren

The Cat Plays With The Mouse

Peter Panter, *Die Schaubühne*,
November 9, 1916

All the soldiers stand in a circle, looking at one fixed point. I approach.

The black and white cat has caught a mouse. Our company's Peter, our black and white cat (a lady cat, however), Peter the First, a young animal, not yet fully grown, but not dainty enough anymore to be taken in hand. The mouse is still full of beans. Peter must have just caught it. Peter has walked around the theater of war for days. Peter has unilaterally distanced itself from the troops, hence, it is hungry, and will soon eat the mouse.

The cat lets the mouse run. The mouse darts away, as if yanked by a string. The cat carefully judges the distance, leaps towards the mouse and holds it down with the tip of its outstretched paw. The mouse struggles. The paw slowly pushes back and forth, the paw is examining the mouse. The cat lies behind its paw and directs everything. But it isn't its paw any more: it is a new animal that has been created for this purpose alone, to be a little more, cruelly more rapid, than the mouse. The paw lifts. The mouse bolts away—it is supposed to bolt away, this is the game. The paw stands over the mouse and strikes it down at the last minute. The mouse squeaks: now the pace becomes livelier.

Hurr... The mouse runs quite a bit. And sits and runs again. The cat sits, and looks into the distance with its

grünen, regungslosen Augen erschreckt ins Weite, als habe sie ein böses Gewissen und befürchte, daß jemand kommt. Jemand – wer sollte kommen? Jetzt läuft die Maus langsamer. Wie eine ›laufende Maus‹, die man kaufen kann: sie wackelt etwas, als ob das Uhrwerk da drinnen schon ein bißchen klapprig wäre. Und wieder hat sie die Katze. Diesmal läßt sie sie nicht los. Sie streichelt sie mit der steifen Pfote; sie streckt sich wohlig aus und schnurrt. Du meine kleine Gefährtin! Es ist fast, als bedaure sie, daß die dumme Maus nicht auch mitspielt. Sie soll irgendetwas tun, die Maus. Die Katze dehnt sich . . . Ich habe sie! ich habe sie! Ach – das ist schön – die Macht, die süße, starke Macht! Ich habe die Oberhand – und sie wird ganz lang vor Behagen, so lang, daß vorn die Kralle abrutscht und Maus entwischt. Es ist nicht mehr viel mit ihr – sie humpelt, fällt auf die Seite, quietscht leise. Wieder hat sie die Katze, aber als sie jetzt losgelassen wird, regt sie sich nicht. Sie ist tot.

Das bringt die Katze außer sich. Wie? Die Maus will nicht mehr? Sie ist nicht mehr lebendig, nicht mehr bei der Sache, kein halb widerwilliges Spielzeug, bei dem der Hauptreiz darin bestand, daß es sich sträubte? Hopp – dann machen wir sie lebendig! Hopp – der Tod hat mir in mein Spiel nichts hereinzuspielen, das sage ich, die Katze! Und packt die Maus mit den Zähnen, schüttelt sie und wirft sie sich über den Kopf und springt hoch in die Luft und fängt sie wieder auf. Die Katze ist toll. Sie rast, sie tobt mit dem kleinen grauen Bündel herum, das sich nicht mehr bewegt, sie tanzt und wälzt sich über die Maus. Dann gibt es einen kleinen Knack; der Höhepunkt ist überschritten, die Katze beginnt erregt, doch schon gedämpft, zu knabbern. Knochen knistern – die Maus wird im Querschnitt dunkelrot – – –.

Aber das ist keine Allegorie. Eine Allegorie ist ein Sinnbild, eine rednerische Form des Vergleichs, ein, wie es heißt, veraltetes Hilfsmittel. Das aber ist Leben – nichts andres als unser

green, unmoving eyes, as if frightened, as if it has a bad conscience and is scared that someone is coming. Who should be coming? Now the mouse runs more slowly, like a wind-up mouse in a store. It wobbles a bit, as if its mechanism is a little decrepit. And again the cat has it, but this time doesn't let go. It strokes the mouse with its stiff paws, stretches our comfortably and purrs. You, my little companion! It is as if it's sorry that the stupid mouse doesn't play along. The mouse should at least do something. The cat stretches—I have it! I have it! Ah, that feels good—power—sweet, strong power! I have the upper hand. And the cat stretches with pleasure, becoming so long that the front claws slide off and the mouse escapes. But there is not much left in the mouse. It limps, falls on its side, and squeaks softly. The cat has it again, but this time when the cat lets go, the mouse doesn't move. It is dead.

But now the cat is exasperated. What—the mouse doesn't want to play any more? The mouse is not alive any more, not involved, no more a half-willing, half-resisting toy, its struggling being its main allure? Hopp! We will bring it back to life. Hopp! Death cannot interfere with my game. Thus say I, the cat. It attacks the mouse with its teeth, shakes it, throws it overhead, jumps high in the air, and catches it again. The cat is mad. It dashes and rages around the small, still, grey bundle that lies there unmoving. It dances and rolls over the mouse. Then there is a sudden small snap, the climax has been reached. The cat starts to nibble, first aroused, then more subdued. Bones crack. The mouse is cut in two: its cross-section is dark red.

But this is no allegory. An allegory is a symbol, a rhetorical form of comparison, if you will, an obsolete tool. But that is life: nothing else but our human conduct. There is

menschliches Tun auch. Es ist kein Unterschied: das war eine Katze, und wir sind Menschen–aber es war doch dasselbe.

Die arme Maus! Vielleicht hätte sie fleißig turnen sollen und allerhand Sport treiben – dann wäre das wohl nicht so schlimm für sie abgelaufen. Oder vielleicht haben ihre Vorfahren gesündigt, die auch einmal Katzen waren und sich dann in Nachdenklichkeit und Milde so langsam zur Maus herunter degenerierten. Wer weiß –.

Die Katze ist eine Sadistin. Aber das ist ein dummes Wort; man denkt dann gleich an eine rothaarige Zirkusgräfin mit hohen Juchtenstiefeln und an verwelkte Mummelgreise im Frack, die ihr die Füße küssen und blödsinnige Komplimente lallen. Nein, so war das gar nicht; das mit der Zirkusgräfin ist nur der letzte Grenzfall.

Natürlich ist die Katze ein Tier wie andre auch. Und sie ist stärker als die Maus, und das hat sie ausgenutzt weit über die Nahrungsfrage hinaus. Sie hatte die Kraft. Und die Maus litt.

Und dieser Schnitt klafft durch alles, dieser Riß spaltet alles – da gibt es keine Brücke. Immer werden sich die zwei gegenüberstehen: die Katze und die Maus.

no difference: that was a cat, we are humans, but we are both the same . . .

The poor mouse! Perhaps its gymnastics should have been better and should have been more sportive—then it would have went better for it. Or perhaps its forefathers have sinned. Perhaps they themselves were once cats: perhaps they degenerated, gradually, meekly, meditatively, into mice? Who knows? –

The cat is a sadist. But that is a stupid word that brings to mind, right away, a red-haired circus countess with high leather boots, and withered old fogies in frock coats who kiss her feet and babble idiotic compliments. No, that is not so: the circus countess is only the worst-case scenario.

Of course, the cat is an animal like any other. And it is also stronger than the mouse, something that it has exploited, above and beyond the question of nutrition. It has the strength, and the mouse suffers.

And this cut gapes in all things, this tear splits everything asunder—no bridge exists. The two will always confront each other. The cat and the mouse.

Kurt Tucholsky

Memento

**Theobald Tiger, *Die Schaubühne*,
3. Oktober 1916, wieder in: *Fromme Gesänge***

Uns Junge hat es umgerissen –
wir stehen draußen so im Feld,
wir glaubten schon, zu halten und zu wissen –
und da versank die ganze Welt.

»Die Welt ist falsch!« Sie ist doch kein Exempel,
wozu der Lehrer seine Lösung hat –
sie ist real und warf uns alle Tempel
und, was wir lieb gehabt, um – wie ein Kartenblatt.

Ihr mahnt den Jüngling, tapfer durchzuhalten.
Gewiß, das scheint ja seine Pflicht –
doch was da in ihm war vom guten, alten,
das gibts in Zukunft alles nicht?

Der neue Wert, die neue Stufenleiter,
der oben und der unten – seltsam Spiel:
Hier gilt die Faust, der Säbel und der Reiter –
das was wir ehren, gilt nicht viel.

Muß das so sein? So darfs nicht bis zur Neige,
nicht bis zum Ende gehn. Wir bleiben rein.
Wir halten durch – es scheint mir gar nicht feige:
Soldat und doch ein Bürger sein!

Sprecht euerm Jungen von der Kriegertugend,
doch davon auch, wenn hart der Panzer klirrt:
Daß er den Träumen seiner Jugend
soll Achtung tragen, wenn er Mann sein wird!

Memento

**Theobald Tiger, *Die Schaubühne*,
October 3, 1916, also in: *Fromme Gesänge***

It threw us boys quite for a loss --
we're standing out there in the field,
thinking to hold on and to know --
and then the world around us fell apart.

'The world is false!' It is not just a problem
For which the teacher has a ready answer--
it is real and brought down all the temples,
and everything we loved, – just like a playing card.

You tell the young man, to be brave, hang on.
And that, it seems, would be his duty clear.
But does the good inside him from before,
not have a place in what is yet to come?

New values – new stepladders leading
all at once both up and down : strange game.
What counts now is the fist, the sabre, and the horseman,
and what we honor doesn't count for much.

Must it be so? It can't go on much longer,
not to the end. We will stay pure.
We'll perservere. It's not the coward's way
to be a soldier and civilian, too.

Tell your youth of all the warrior's virtues,
But tell him, too, amid the clashing steel,
that all his youthful dreams as well
must have their due, if he would be a man!

Kurt Tucholsky

Das Grammophon

Peter Panter, *Simplicissimus*, 3. October 1916

Wenn die Musik der Liebe Nahrung ist
Gebt volles Maß! –

Wir haben jetzt im Unterstand auch ein Grammophon. Am Tage geht es hier, im Geschäftszimmer der Kompanie, ernst und sachlich zu. Aber abends, wenn die Meldungen erstattet sind, wenn das Telefon nicht mehr summt, wenn der ganze Hallo vorbei und verrauscht ist, dann setzt einer die Membrane auf, das Ding räuspert sich, krächzt... und los gehts.

Das Programm ist schon ganz respektabel. Was die leichtgeschürzte Muse angeht, so brillieren da zunächst die Männerquartette, solche, die sonntags nachmittags viere lang mit üppigen Zylinderhüten und weißen Glacisten vor die erstaunte Zuhörerschaft treten, der Tenor knufft den Bariton in die Seite und sagt: »I muaß dir was sag'n!« – und dann sagt ers, aber auf tenorisch: »I hab amal an Rausch g'habt...« Der Flügelmann von rechts ist ein schwitzender Dicker, er bläst sich ganz auf, und in der Tiefe kocht ihm ein mächtiger Baß.

Man sieht das nicht? Wir rauchen, und wir sehen das. Instrumentalsoli sind da, weinende Celli, klappernde Xylophone und ein Mann, der die Vöglein im Walde gar lieblich nachahmt. Wir haben Potpourris: wenn ein Lied zu Ende ist, schlägt der Mann am Klavier einfach den Septimenakkord der nächsthöheren Tonart an, und die Überleitung ist fertig. Und wir haben die Märsche –! Die Märsche mit dem ganzen Kling, klang, gloria und dem zuckenden Rhythmus des Vier-

The Gramophone

Peter Panter, *Simplicissimus*, October 3, 1916

If music be the food of love, Play on
(Shakespeare, Twelfth Night)

We have a gramophone in our dugout. During the day, everything is serious and business-like in our orderly room. But in the evening when communications are reported, the telephone does not hum any more, when the whole business of the day is over and faded away, then someone puts the machine on, the thing coughs and cracks, and the party begins.

The program is quite respectable. As far as the scantily clad Muse is concerned, first the male quartets shine, like four performers on Sunday afternoon with plush toppers and white gloves parading before an amazed audience. The tenor pokes the baritone in the side and says: 'I mus' tell you somethin''—and then he says it, in tenor: 'Once I was boozed up.'—The wingman on the right is sweaty and fat: he blows himself up, and in the depths a powerful bass boils up.

Don't you see it? We smoke, and we see it all. The instrument solos are there, the weeping celli, clattering xylophone, and a man who imitates birds in the woods just swell. We have potpourris: when a song ends, the pianist simply plays the seventh chord of the next highest key, and the transition is complete. And there are the marches—! The marches with all their kling klang gloria, and the jerky, whipping rhythm of four-four time.

vierteltaktes. Das Schönste aber an ihnen sind die Trios: wie da in einer scheinbar weichen Melodie die verhaltene Kraft liegt, die nur einmal einen Augenblick nachläßt, sich entspannt – aber sie ist doch da – es ist, wie wenn jemand nach Monaten wieder in einem Federbett sich wohlig streckt . . .

Aber wir haben auch ernste Musik. Mächtige Gesänge von Wagner: wir stoben auseinander, als das erste Mal eine ungeheure Stimme aus dem kleinen Kasten herausbrüllte: »Ach, Elsa, nur ein Jahr –!« Und auch der Abendstern erglänzt uns weit hinaus. Einer ist da, der ist unmusikalisch wie ein Roß; ich habe nie geglaubt, daß Musik ihn überhaupt berühren könnte – aber er legte die Hände wohlig über den Bauch bei Zugehörbringung obgenannten Abendsterns. Ja, ja . . . der Wagner . . . Und wenn der Sänger seine Tränen aus der Kehle hat rinnen lassen, dann singt die fette Primadonna mit dem hochbezahlten Sopran. »Draußen am Wall bei Sevilla« – es ist geradezu ketzerisch, wie frech dieses Weib die Töne heraustrillert. Sieh, und vor den dunkelroten Samtvorhang tritt ein blasser Mensch – ›Bajatscho‹, wie der Feldwebel, wohl in Anlehnung an seine italienische Hochzeitsreise, zu sagen pflegt – und tut uns kund, daß er mit dem Gesichte zwar lache, innen aber sei er ein Meer von Blut und Tränen. Und so wirbelt das durcheinander – Polkas, mit einer belfernden Klarinette – Hochzeitsmärsche ziehn vorüber, kleine Chöre singen Braut –, beziehungsweise Trauermärsche, und auf blaßblauem Hintergrund wiegt sich eine bonbonrosa Blüte: der Faustwalzer. Sicher ist auch sonst noch allerhand Erzfeindliches unter den Platten – aber hier draußen ist man damit nicht so ängstlich.

Wenn es aber ganz spät geworden ist, dann hole ich meine Privatplatte heraus. Sie ist doppelseitig bespielt: auf der einen Seite trägt sie einen nun schon leicht angejahrten Modewalzer. Er hat den Gegentakt, ist sehr schwer zu tanzen und wird von einem kleinen Orchesterchen

But the most beautiful are the trios: how their subdued power lies in an apparently delicate melody, which ceases for a moment, slackens—but is still there—it is like one who, after many months, stretches comfortably in a feather-bed.

But there is also serious music. Powerful Wagner chorales: we scatter apart when a huge voice roars out of the small box for the first time. 'Oh Elsa, only a year at your side –!' (Lohengrin). And also the evening star shines way beyond (Tannhäuser). One of us is as unmusical as a horse: I never would have thought that music would move him at all—but he puts his hands comfortably over his belly upon being exposed to said evening star. Yes, yes, Wagner . . . And when the singer sings with tears running from his throat, when the fat prima donna, with the highly paid soprano voice, sings 'near the walls of Seville' (Carmen), it is downright heretical how sassily the woman warbles out the notes. And look, a pale man stands in front of the dark red silk curtain,—"Bajatscho," as the sergeant used to call him, probably in remembrance of what he picked up on his honeymoon in Italy—, and he tells us that he laughs with his face only and that inside he is a sea of blood and tears. And so everything whirls together—polkas, with a bellowing clarinet, wedding marches pass by, small choirs sing wedding marches—respectively funeral marches—, and on a pale blue background a pink blossom: the Faust waltz. All sorts of arch enemies surely lurk amongst the records—but here in the field one is not so worried about them.

But when it becomes really late, then I take my private record out. It has music on both sides. On one side there is a slightly dated waltz: it is written in counter-rhythm, is very difficult to dance to, and is played by a small orchestra with discrete orchestration. By then it is usually

gespielt, mit feiner diskreter Besetzung. Das ist meist so gegen zwölf Uhr, der Rauch beißt in die Augen. – Es ist alles so leicht und angenehm und mühelos, wie wenn man in einem schönen weißen Dampfer flußab fährt. Und die Kapelle spielt, nur für mich allein, in memoriam.

Und auf der anderen Seite – es ist eigentlich gar nichts weiter zu erzählen. In dem Vorstadttheater spielten sie damals ein ergreifendes Stück mit Gesang und Tanz. Weil der Raum so groß war wie ein Reitstall, hatte der Herr Regisseur die Schauspieler sicherlich auf der Probe angewiesen, auch den Fünfzig-Pfennig-Plätzen das ihrige zukommen zu lassen. Und ob sie ließen! – Der Fürst brüllte, daß wir in unserer Zwei-Mark-fünfunddreißig-Pfennig-Loge fast von den Stühlen fielen. Und es brüllte die Prinzessin, und der alte Graf schrie, bis er fast platzte, und es brüllte der Intrigant und das junge Liebespaar und alle, alle. Und im Laufe der traurigen Begebenheiten sang Miss Elvira auch dieses Lied, das der Kasten nun spielt. Horch –!

Ich stehe hier ganz alleine,

ich bin eine Bettlerin – – –

Sie hatte ein Armband um das schlanke Bein und war sicher ein gefälliges Mädchen. Und neben mir saß die Claire, voll Übermut, wie wir damals waren, und brachte durch ihre Existenz beinahe die ganze Kapelle aus dem Takt. Durch die Türen des gräflichen Zimmers hindurch sahen wir die Kulissenschieber ihr Bier trinken – und wir waren so glücklich damals und so vergnügt, wie heute nur noch in der Erinnerung, und das will etwas heißen.

Der Kasten hat geendigt. Wir rauchen noch immer. Jeder sieht in die Kerzen.

Sie schreiben jetzt so viel von nationaler Wiedergeburt. Es war sicherlich nicht alles so, wie es sein sollte. Aber was sie jetzt zu Hause aus uns herausdestillieren wollen – – – Also so sollen wir werden? So völkisch, so schauerlich

around midnight, smoke bites into my eyes—everything is so light and effortless, like travelling downstream on a white steamboat. And the ensemble plays for me alone, in memoriam.

And on the other side—there is really nothing more to tell. Back in the day, they played a poignant piece, with song and dance, in the suburban theater. Because the room was as big as a riding stable, the honorable director surely instructed the actors during the rehearsal to make sure the cheap fifty pfennig seats have fun too. And how they did it!—The prince hollered so loudly on the stage that we almost fell from the chairs in our two mark thirty-five boxes. And the princess howled and the old duke yelled until he almost burst, and the schemer bawled, and the young pair of lovers, and everyone else. And in the course of the sad events Miss Elvira also sang this song that the box now plays (opera/operetta unknown). Listen –!

I remain here all alone,

I am a beggar – – –

She had an armband around her slender leg, and was surely a pleasing young girl. And next to me sat Claire, full of cockiness as she was then, and by her presence almost brought the entire ensemble out of rhythm. Through the door of the count's chamber we saw the stage hands drinking beer—and we were so happy and merry in this time like only in our memory today, and that means a lot.

The record has finished. We are still smoking. Each of us stares into the candles.

They write so much about national rebirth now. Things were certainly not all as they should have been in the past. But what the folks back home want to distill out of us now – – – So, this is what we are supposed to become? So

begeistert, so voll zager Fröhlichkeit, wie man es allenfalls Schülern in der Freiviertelstunde gestattet? Ich glaube, hier draußen tut jeder, was er kann. Und freut sich, wenn er eine kleine Abwechslung hat, die ihn an seinen Platz zu Hause erinnert und an sein Wesen und sein Wirken, seine Heimat und seine Welt. Und er denkt sich wohl so, wie er dies und jenes besser machen könnte, wenn er wieder nach Hause kommt.

Aber die nationale Wiedergeburt – – – Da können wir doch nichts Festes versprechen.

nationalistically and nightmarishly enthusiastic, so full of subdued gaiety, like the one permitted schoolchildren in their fifteen-minute break? I believe that here in the field each man does what he can, and is happy when he has a small diversion, which reminds him of his place at home and his existence, his actions, his native country, his world. And he thinks how he can make this and that better when he returns home.

But as for national rebirth – – – we can promise nothing for sure.

German soldiers in a railroad car on the way to the front during early World War I, taken in 1914. A message on the car spells out "Trip to Paris"; early in the war all sides expected the conflict to be a short one.
Picture source: Unknown

Kurt Tucholsky

Der Kriegslieferant

Theobald Tiger, *Die Schaubühne*, 14. Dezember 1916

Du wohnst irgendwo am Friedrichshaine.
Auf deiner Ehe ruhte Gottes Segen
(sechs Kinder). Deine säuerlichen Weine
ernährten nebst Versicherungsverträgen
den Renntips, auch wohl einem Spielchen „Meine
und Deine Tante" dich noch allerwegen.[*]
Bald hattst du nichts, bald hattst du blaue Scheine.
Oft sah man deine Frau die Treppe fegen.

Doch als der Welt vor Angst die Pulse stocken,
wirfst du dich auf die Marke „Suppenkraft" –
Da stieg dein Stern! In der Gemahlin Locken
blitzt die Agraffe auf dem Band von Taft.

Von Paulchen Thumann, Stöwer und Van Gocken[†]
Hast du dir schnell das nötigste errafft.
Und läuten einmal uns die Friedensglocken:
Was kost' Berlin? – Du hast das Ding geschafft!

---

[*] "Meine und Deine Tante" is a card game, where luck alone determines who will win, comparable to the American game "War" "Blaue Scheine" refers to the color of the 100 Mark notes in the German Reich. The U.S equivalent is $100, also known as Benjamins.
[†] Paul Thumann and Willy Stöwer were now-forgotten German artists, and so was, most likely, Van Gocken.

The War Contractor

Theobald Tiger, *Die Schaubühne,*
December 14, 1916

You live someplace in Friedrichshain
And God has showered blessings on your marriage
(six children). And your sour wines together
with what you got from selling life insurance,
some racing tips, and playing "war" for money
kept you and yours in bread up to this point.
By times you were broke, by times you had piles of Benjamins.
We often saw your wife sweeping the staircase.

But when the world from dreadful fear stops breathing
You bet it all on your brand "Super Soup" –
Your ships came in! In your wife's stylish locks now
sparkle baubles on a silken band.

From Paulchen Thumann, Stöwer and Van Gocken
You've quickly grabbed the stuff you need.
And when at last the peace bells ring for others:
What price Berlin? You've got it made, old friend!*

---

* Berliners often lived in five story walk-ups and someone had to keep the staircase orderly. This was either the super, or, as in this case, a resident looking to earn a little exra money. The up and down of the staircase is itself a metaphor for the protagonist's finances before he hits on Super Soup.

Kurt Tucholsky

Zum ersten August

Theobald Tiger, *Die Weltbühne*, 1. August 1918

Herr Krieg, du bist unsre Zuflucht für und für.

Ehe die Berge wurden und die Länder und die Welt geschaffen wurden, warst du, Krieg, von Ewigkeit zu Ewigkeit.

Der du die andern Menschen lässest sterben und sprichst: Hinweg, Menschenkinder!

Denn vier Jahre sind vor dir wie der Tag, der gestern vergangen ist, und wie eine Nachtwache.

Du lässest sie dahinfahren wie einen Strom, und sie sind zum Glück wie ein Schlaf; gleichwie ein Gras, das doch bald welk wird.

Das machet dein Zorn, daß sie so vergehen, und dein Grimm, daß sie, sie, sie so dahin müssen.

Denn ihre Missetaten stellest du vor dich, ihre Sünden ins Licht vor deinem Angesichte.

Ihr Leben währet zwanzig Jahre, und wenns hochkommt, so sinds fünfundzwanzig, und wenns köstlich gewesen ist, so ist es schnell dahingefahren, als flögen sie davon.

Wer glaubts noch nicht, daß du so sehr zürnest? und wer fürchtet sich noch nicht vor solchem deinem Grimm?

Lehre sie bedenken, daß sie sterben müssen, auf daß wir klug werden.

Zeige deinen Knechten deine Werke und deine Ehre ihren Kindern.

Und der KRIEG, unser Gott, sei uns freundlich und fördere das Werk unsrer Hände; ja, das Werk unsrer Hände wolle er fördern!

Prayer After the Slaughter

August First

Theobald Tiger, *Die Weltbühne*, August 1, 1918

Lord War, you are our refuge now and forever.

 Before the mountains were brought forth and the lands and the world created, you, war, were from everlasting to everlasting.

 You who allow other people to die, all the while saying: be gone, children of men!

 Four years to you are like one yesterday, like standing watch for a single night.

 You let them continue on, like a river, and they are, thank goodness, like sleep; just like the grass, which soon withers.

 Your rage is the reason that they perish thus, and your fury, that they, they, they must pass away.

 For you recall all of their misdeeds, turn the spotlight on their sins before your face.

 Their life lasts twenty years, or, if they are strong, twenty-five years, and if sweet, then soon complete, as if they'd flown away.

 Do any not believe, that you're so very angry? and who has not yet learned to fear your awful rage?

 Teach them to recall that they must die so that we might become wise.

 Show your slaves your works and your honor to their children.

 And may WAR, our God, be friendly and bless the work of our hands; yes, the work of our hands may he bless!

This poem is a riff on Psalm 90: A prayer of Moses, the man of God.

Kolonne

Theobald Tiger, *Berliner Tageblatt*, 14. Oktober 1918

Hochrädrige, überdachte Wagen.
Immer einer hinter dem andern.
Der Regen rieselt. Sie fahren seit Tagen,
Seit Wochen im Schritt, ein endloses Wandern.
Die Fahrer drösen auf ihren Böcken,
Vorne im Halbschlaf der Herr Sergeant;
Das Wasser rinnt an den schweren Röcken
Herunter – grau und glatt liegt das Land – –
Der Fahrer träumt auf seinem Sitze,
Nur manchmal schreckt ein Rufen den Mann.
Ein Ruf pflanzt sich fort von hinten zur Spitze
„Rechts ran!"

Ein Auto braust. Vorbei. Sie sinnen
Und träumen wieder im gleichen Trott.
Wie wird das draußen? Wie wird das drinnen?
Friede? Wandlung? Du lieber Gott!
Solange geschmäht – jetzt steht es kritisch –
Der Rote war stets ein schwarzer Mann –
Jäh fährt er auf. Wie klingt das politisch:
„Rechts ran!"

Wird sich das ändern? In neuen Bahnen?
Es wäre die allerhöchste Zeit.
Nicht mehr: Obrigkeit. Untertanen,
Nur noch Deutsche – im gleichen Leid.
Die Pferde poltern ein wenig geschwinder,

The Convoy

Theobald Tiger, *Berliner Tageblatt*, October 14, 1918

A long line of high-wheeled covered wagons,
Always one and then one more behind.
The rain beats down. They've been out here for days.
For weeks at a walk, a never-ending drift
The draymen twiddle thumbs in their boxes,
Up front the Sergeant is half-asleep;
The rain runs down on their heavy coats and
Soaks them—the land lies grey and flat –
In his seat the drayman sits dreaming,
But sometimes a call shakes him awake.
A call from the back heard right through to the front:
"Move right!"

A car roars by. It's gone. They're thinking,
And dreaming again just like before.
How is it out there? How will it be here?
Peace time? Changes? God only knows!
So long reviled—it's a critical time –
The Reds were always seen as black hats –
He jerks awake. Sounds like politics that:
"Move right!"

Will things be different? In this new era?
It would certainly be about time.
No aristocrats or underlings,
Only Germans—shared suffering.
The horses clatter a little bit faster,

Sein nasses Gesicht zieht sich lustig in Falten:
Nur noch Landsleute – und die Kinder
Haben's besser als ihre Alten.
Neue Zeiten und neue Besen –
Besser, als er es je haben kann . . .
So ist es denn nicht umsonst gewesen:
„Links ran!"

Prayer After the Slaughter

Now merry wrinkles appear on his face;
Only our people left—and the children
Have it better than their old folks did.
New times have come, new brooms are sweeping –
Better than even he could have hoped . . .
So then it was at least not all in vain:
"Move left!"

An assault by the French army on German positions; against the German infantry, not depicted here. Picture taken in Champagne, France, 1917.
Picture source: Unknown

Helm ab –!

Theobald Tiger, *Die Weltbühne,*
28. November 1918

Da liegt die große Pickelhaube
Im schwarzen, dunkeln Grabesloch.
Sie ruhe sanft ... Sieh da, ich glaube,
sie wackelt noch.

Ein Landrat fletscht die großen Zähne:
„Am Grabe noch ein Spottgedicht?
De mortuis nil nisi bene!"
Ich weiß doch nicht.

Steigt unser Leid heut zu den Sternen
Nach blutigem Kling-Klang-Gloria –
Vergeßt es nicht: Ihr sollt das lernen,
wie es geschah.

Vergeßt sie nicht: die Ordensritter,
den Heimatkistenoffizier,
die Jungs der Reklamiertenzither –
all das Getier.

Helm ab!
Voll Pietät? Ja, Kuchen!
Er liegt auf wohlverdientem Mist.
Wir müssen erst dem Alten fluchen
Und dann nach gutem Neuen suchen –
Bis er vermodert ist.

Helmet Off—!

Theobald Tiger, *Die Weltbühne*, November 28, 1918

There the great spiked helmet lies
In a black, dark hole of a grave.
May it rest easy. . . But look, I think
It's wobbling still.

A district head bares his large teeth
"Must this graveside satire be?
De mortuis nil nisi bene!"
I'm not sure.

As our pain rises to the stars,
And bloody bing-bang-glory fades –
Do not forget! You all should learn
How we got here.

Forget them not: the knighted orders,
The petty local officers
the whining choir of 4-F boys –
Animals all.

Helmet off!
Feeling pious? Not a bit!
It lies on well-deserved shit.
First off we have to curse the old
Then look for something new and good –
Until it rots away.

Weihnachten

Kaspar Hauser, *Die Weltbühne*, 19. Dezember 1918, again in: *Fromme Gesänge*

So steh ich nun vor deutschen Trümmern
und sing mir still mein Weihnachtslied.
Ich brauch mich nicht mehr drum zu kümmern,
was weit in aller Welt geschieht.
Die ist den andern. Uns die Klage.
Ich summe leis, ich merk es kaum,
die Weise meiner Jugendtage:
O Tannebaum!

Wenn ich so der Knecht Ruprecht wäre
und käm in dies Brimborium
– bei Deutschen fruchtet keine Lehre –
weiß Gott! ich kehrte wieder um.
Das letzte Brotkorn geht zur Neige.
Die Gasse grölt. Sie schlagen Schaum.
Ich hing sie gern in deine Zweige,
O Tannebaum!

Ich starre in die Knisterkerzen:
Wer ist an all dem Jammer schuld?
Wer warf uns so in Blut und Schmerzen?
Uns Deutsche mit der Lammsgeduld?
Die leiden nicht. Die warten bieder.
Ich träume meinen alten Traum:
Schlag, Volk, den Kastendünkel nieder!
Glaub diesen Burschen nie, nie wieder!
Dann sing du frei die Weihnachtslieder:
O Tannebaum! O Tannebaum!

Christmas

Kaspar Hauser, *Die Weltbühne*, December 19, 1918, again in: *Fromme Gesänge*

So now I face the German ruins
and softly sing my Christmas song.
I need not worry any more
what happens in the wider world.
It is their problem. Ours is mourning.
I softly hum, I barely hear
the tune I sang when I was young:
O Christmas Tree!

Let's say I were to be Knecht Ruprecht
and ended up in all this fuss
--with Germans doctrines don't bear fruit—
God knows, I'd turn around at once.
Soon now the last crumb will be gone.
The streets are restless. They are frothing.
I'd love to hang them on your branches,
O Christmas Tree!

I watch the candles as they sputter:
Whose fault is all this misery?
Who cast us into blood and pain?
We Germans with our lamb-like patience?
They suffer not. They calmly wait.
I dream again my dream of yore:
crush the snobbery of class!
Don't ever trust these guys again!
Then sing out free the Christmas carols:
O Christmas Tree! O Christmas Tree!

Zwei Erschlagene

Kaspar Hauser, *Die Weltbühne,* 23. Januar 1919, wieder in: *Fromme Gesänge*

Märtyrer . . . ? Nein.
Aber Pöbelsbeute.
Sie wagtens. Wie selten ist das heute.
Sie packten zu, und sie setzten sich ein:
Sie wollten nicht nur Theoretiker sein.

Er: ein Wirrkopf von mittleren Maßen.
Er suchte das Menschenheil in den Straßen.
Armer Kerl: es liegt nicht da.
Er tat das Seine, wie er es sah.
Er wollte die Unterdrückten heben,
er wollte für sie ein menschliches Leben.
Sie haben den Idealisten betrogen,
den Meergott verschlangen die eigenen Wogen.
Sie knackten die Kassen, der Aufruhr tollt –
Armer Kerl, hast du das gewollt?

Sie: der Mann von den zwei Beiden.
Ein Leben voll Hatz und Gefängnisleiden.
Hohn und Spott und schwarz-weiße Chikane
Und dennoch treu der Fahne, der Fahne!
Und immer wieder: Haft und Gefängnis
Und Spitzeljagd und Landratsbedrängnis.
Und immer wieder: Gefängnis und Haft –
Sie hatte die stärkste Manneskraft.

Die Parze des Rinnsteins zerschnitt die Fäden.
Da liegen die Beiden am Hotel Eden.

Two Clubbed to Death

Kaspar Hauser, *Die Weltbühne,*
January 23, 1919, again in: *Fromme Gesänge*

Martyrs were they . . .? No.
But victims of the rabble.
They risked it. How rare is that today.
The rolled up their sleeves and they got involved:
Theory by itself was not enough at all.

He: a muddled fellow of average build
He looked in the streets to find our salvation.
Poor sad soul: it lies not there.
He did what he could, as he saw it.
He wanted to lift up the oppressed,
They, too, should fulfill their human existence.
But they all betrayed their idealist champion,
His own waves devoured the sea-god who called them.
They broke the banks open, the riot spread—
Poor sad soul, did you want this instead?

She: the one who had the pants on.
A life on the run or spent wasting in jail.
Mockery, scorn and conservative harrassment,
But ever faithful to the flag, to the flag!
Over and over arrested and jailed!
The prey of informers and official hounding.
Over and over arrested and jailed! –
She had the strength of the strongest man.

The Fate of the Gutter cut off their life threads.
There both of them lie by the Hotel Eden.

Bestellte Arbeit? Die Bourgeoisie?
So tatkräftig war die gute doch nie ...
Wehrlos wurden zwei Menschen erschlagen

Und es kreischen Geier die Totenklagen:
Gott sei Dank! Vorbei ist die Not!
„Man schlug", schreibt Eriner, „die Galizierin tot!"
Wir atmen auf! Hurra Bourgeoisie!
Jetzt spiele dein Spielchen ohne die!

Nicht ohne! Man kann die Körper zerschneiden.
Aber das eine bliebt von den Beiden:

Wie man sich selber die Treue hält,
wie man gegen eine feindliche Welt
mit reinem Schilde streiten kann,
das vergißt den Beiden kein ehrlicher Mann!

Wir sind, weiß Gott, keine Spartaciden.
Ehre zwei Kämpfern!
Sie ruhen in Frieden!

Prayer After the Slaughter

A contract job? The Bourgeoisie?
She never was so energetic before . . .
The two were clubbed down; they could not resist.

And vultures screech out the funeral dirges:
Thanks be to God! The danger is gone!
One wrote: 'They struck the Galician dead!'
We're free to breathe! Hurrah Bourgeoisie!
Now your games can go on without them!

Not without! You can cut their bodies to pieces
But one thing remains, that both of them had.

How to stay faithful to your own self,
How to stand up to a world full of foes
And shield yourself with a pure cause –
No honest man can forget to thank them for that.

God knows we want no part of Spartacide.
Honor two warriors!!
They rest in peace!*

---

* The poem refers to the murders of Rosa Luxemburg and Karl Liebknecht. Luxemburg, a Polish-Jewish immigrant to Germany, was the founder of the anti-war Spartakusbund (Spartacus League) which eventually became the Communist Party of Germany (KPD), together with Liebknecht. Liebknecht, a staunch opponent of WWI, declared the Freie Sozialistische Republik (Free Socialist Republic) from a balcony of the Berlin Castle, two hours after Philipp Scheidemann's declaration of a German Republic from a balcony of the Reichstag in 1919. They were both murdered by Freikorps men, World War I veterans banded together in right-wing paramilitary groups. Luxemburg's body was thrown into the Landwehr Canal in Berlin.

Militaria
›Unser Militär‹

Ignaz Wrobel
Die Weltbühne, 20. Februar 1919

*Das rekelt sich und gähnt und sauft und hurt
und tut (versteht sich) Dienst voll Zucht und Strenge.
Ein Lustspiel von der Menge für die Menge.
So sieht Welt aus vor der Person Geburt.*
—Christian Morgenstern

Die Offiziere tragen immer Handschuhe, wenn sie auch schmutzig sind.
Regiebemerkung zu einem Theaterstück

Wir haben in den vorigen Heften der ›Weltbühne‹ betrachtet, wie es in der deutschen Armee zugegangen ist: ein trüber Haufe voller Qual und Greuel, Weltenklüfte zwischen Offizier und Mann, Unterschlagung und Diebstähle von Lebensmitteln zugunsten der höhern Ränge, Requisitionen ohne Ziel und Maß, falsche Schwäche und falsche Härte den fremden Landeseinwohnern gegenüber, Vaterländischer Unterricht, Mantel der Lüge über all den Jammer und alle Verbrechen: ›Unser Militär‹. Aber unbeirrbar steht der deutsche Spießer, nein, der deutsche Bürger da, der Patriot quand-même er wirft sich in die Brust. Aber der Deutsche, der nichts gesehen hat, und als seien Krieg und Zusammenbruch nicht gewesen, ruft er stolz tönend in die Lüfte: »Unser Militär!«
 Wie ist das zu erklären? Wie kann ein Volk gedeutet wer-

Militaria
'Our Military'

Ignaz Wrobel
Die Weltbühne, Februray 20, 1919

It stinks and yawns and drinks and whores
But thinks that it is Duty: cultured, strict.
A comedy that's by and for the crowds.
The world looks so before the man is born.

—Christian Morgenstern

Our officers wear gloves even when they are dirty.
Directions for a play.

In a previous issue of *Die Weltbühne*, we have observed the conditions in the German Army: a gloomy horde full of anguish and horror, chasms of difference between officers and men, embezzlement and theft of provisions for the higher ranks, requisitioning without goal and measure, false weakness and false harshness against the foreign populations in the guise of education about the Fatherland, a cloak of lies over all suffering and crimes; -- yes, that is 'Our Military.' But nevertheless there stands the German bourgeois, the citizen and patriot, as he is, puffed up with his own self-importance. Herman the German, who has seen nothing, proudly proclaiming as if war and collapse had not occurred: 'Our Military!.'

How can this be explained? How can one explain a peo-

den, das nach allem, was geschehen ist, nach allem, was es erfahren und gelitten hat, den verlorenen Krieg als einen kleinen Betriebsunfall ansieht – »Reden wir nicht weiter darüber!« –, und das heute, heute am liebsten das alte böse Spiel von damals wieder aufnehmen möchte: die Unterdrückung durch aufgeblasene Vorgesetzte, ein Deutscher tritt den andern und ist stolz, ihn zu treten, die schimmernden vergötterten Abzeichen, der Götze Leutnant – »unser Militär!« Wie ist das zu erklären?

Die militaristische Schande Deutschlands ist nur möglich gewesen, weil sie die tiefsten und schlechtesten Instinkte des Volkes befriedigt hat.

Der Deutsche läßt sich für jede Arbeit, die er gewissenhaft und gut verrichten soll, mit Respekt überzahlen. Er arbeitet, aber er will dafür ästimiert werden. Ich sage absichtlich nicht ›geachtet‹ – daran liegt ihm gar nichts. Er will ästimiert werden; das Schartekenwort besagt: man soll den Hut vor ihm ziehen und das Maul ehrfurchtsvoll aufsperren. Er tritt dann aus seinem kleinen Bürgerdasein heraus, wie Heinrich Mann das in der Bibel des Wilhelminischen Zeitalters, im ›Untertan‹, formuliert hat: »Er genoß einen der Augenblicke, in denen er mehr bedeutete als sich selbst und im Geiste eines Höheren handelte.«

Der Soldat hat dafür das Wort: »Dienst ist Dienst, und Schnaps ist Schnaps« erfunden – aber es war doch Schnapsdienst, der da herauskam.

Der Wurm, der an aller Herzen fraß, war eine ungeheure, lächerliche Selbstüberschätzung in der Arbeit. Ob Architekt oder Bürovorsteher, Eisenbahnassistent oder Apotheker, Oberlehrer oder Prinzipal – sie alle waren beseligt, einmal, ach, nur ein einziges Mal, auf einen andern heruntersehen zu können, und wär es auch nur ein Laufbursche gewesen.

Dieser unselige Drang feierte Orgien im deutschen Heer. Da wurde einem kein neues Amt übertragen – da wurde

ple who, after everything that has happened, after everything that they have experienced and suffered, regard the lost war as a small occupational accident? -- 'Let us not speak of it anymore!.' What to do with a nation who today, this very day, would love to commence the previous old, dirty game: the oppression by puffed up superiors, one German kicking another, proud to have done so, the shimmering, deified insignia, the tin god lieutenant—'Our Military!' How can this be explained?

Germany's military disgrace was only possible because it satisfied the deepest and most basic instincts of the people.

A German wishes to be overly regarded for any work that he does conscientiously and well. He works, but he wants to be held in esteem for it. I purposely do not say 'respected'—this means nothing to him. He wishes to be esteemed. As the stupid old saying goes: 'one must take off one's hat to him and reverently open one's mouth wide.' He then escapes from his petty bourgeois existence, as Heinrich Mann has described in the bible of the Wilhelmine period *Der Untertan* (The Loyal Subject); 'he enjoyed one of the moments when he rises above himself, and acted in the spirit of someone higher.'

The soldier usually says: 'Service is service, and Schnapps is Schnapps.' But out of this came only Schnapps-service.

The worm that gnawed at every heart was enormous, laughable work hubris. Architect or office head, railway assistant or pharmacist, senior teacher or principal –all were overtly happy if once, even only once, they could look down on someone else, even if he was only a delivery boy.

This deplorable compulsion was celebrated orgiastically in the German Army. There, no new office was 'assigned,

einer ›befördert‹: Gottlieb Schulze wachte eines Tages auf und war Oberschulze und Herr und Gebieter über die Seelen seiner Mitschulzen. Da blühten die giftigsten Früchte. Da konnte der Vizefeldwebel dem Unteroffizier, der Major dem Hauptmann eins auswischen, ohne daß der Gescholtene muckste: der Dienst! der Dienst! Rangerhöhung färbte noch auf die Familie ab; welcher Stolz, wenn ein Medizinmann der Gattin zeigte: »Der Mann da drüben ist mein Unterarzt!« Seiner . . . Und diese Wallenstein-Pose behielten alle bei, davon lebten sie; sie taten, als hätten sie ›ihre Leute‹ angeworben, als folgten die freiwillig dem erkorenen Führer. Und hinter den alten Ritterkulissen schacherten und betrogen wildgewordene Kaufleute und Beamte.

Muß das sein? Werden wir ewig Vaterlandsliebe mit Patriotismus, Ordnung mit Kadavergehorsam, Pünktlichkeit mit Sklaverei, jedes Ding mit seiner Karikatur überzahlen müssen? Gibt es zwischen Schludrigkeit und dem berüchtigten preußischen Unteroffizier kein Mittelding?

Es gibt eines, und in ihm liegt das Heil der Welt und die Genesung dieses unglücklichen, verblendeten Landes. Und es heißt: Sachlichkeit.

Der Sturm ist vorübergebraust – der deutsche Spitzweg-Bürger steckt die Nase zum Fenster heraus, dann den ganzen Kopf und spricht frohbewegt: »Aber es regnet ja gar nicht mehr!« Und nimmt den alten Stock und den alten Hut . . .

Schlagt sie ihm herunter! Laßt nie, nie wieder diese Burschen aufkommen, die euch gemartert haben und gequält und gedemütigt und kujoniert!

Sie zittern und gieren auf den Augenblick, da eine neue Kompromißregierung das neue Volksheer errichtet – ›natürlich nur ein geordnetes Heerwesen mit festen Befehlsverhältnissen‹. Selbstverständlich. Sie pfeifen auf alle Prinzipien. Sie stehen auf dem Boden des neuen Staates. Und der Unteroffizier wird wieder den Rekruten ins Kreuz tre-

'it was rather 'promoted.' Gottlieb Schulze woke up one day and was Senior Schulze, lord and master over the soul of his other Schulzes. The most poisonous fruits bloomed. The staff sergeant could score off the corporal, the major off the captain, without the person being insulted moving a muscle: 'Duty! Service!.' Promotion rubbed off onto the family. What pride when a physician showed his spouse: 'That man over there is my junior doctor!' Yeah, his . . .

And this Wallenstein pose was retained by all: they lived off it. They acted as if they had hired 'their people,' as if they followed their chosen leader. And hidden behind the ancient knight's scenery businessmen and public servants turned crazy were haggling and cheating.

Must it be this way? Will we always have to overpay our love of Fatherland with patriotism, order with corpse-like obedience, and punctuality with slavery, everything with its caricature? Is there no middle way between sloppiness and the notorious Prussian non-commissioned officer?

There is one solution, and in it lies the salvation of the world and that of this unhappy, blinded country. It is called objectivity.

The storm has roared past—the German petty-bourgeois first sticks his nose, then his whole head, out of the window, and says joyfully: 'But it isn't raining anymore!' He takes his old stick and old hat . . .

Strike them away from him! Never, never let these buggers who have martyred, tortured, humiliated and bullied you resurface!

They tremble, and lust for the moment when a new coalition government founds the new militia army—'naturally only an ordered army with firm chains of command.' Obviously. They whistle at all principles. They stand on the ground of the new state. And the non-commissioned officer will again wreak vengeance

ten – natürlich auf demokratischer Grundlage. Aber diesmal treten wir wieder.

Wir erwarten gar nicht, daß eine Generation, die nur leben konnte, wenn sie sich maßlos eitel und aufgebläht in ihrer Arbeit überschätzen und vergöttern ließ, den alten Schleppsäbel abtut und vernünftig und menschlich wird. Sie ist unheilbar. Wir wollen ihr die Untertanen entziehen. Wir wollen, daß es keine Menschen mehr gibt, die sich gefallen lassen, was jene mit der Miene der Gottähnlichkeit verhängten. Wir sind frei.

Wir warens nicht. Wie jämmerlich die Einwände, wie spießig der läppischste von allen: »Man darf nicht verallgemeinern.« Und doch war alles so gemein . . .

Freilich: dem ist nicht mit Gerichtsverhandlungen beizukommen. Als damals Rosa Luxemburg von den Soldatenmißhandlungen schrieb, da sperrten sie sie ein, weil sie nicht gerichtsnotorisch machen konnte, was sich in abgesperrten Kasernenhöfen an Bestialitäten abgespielt hatte. Aber nie wird sonnenklar zu beweisen sein, was mit so viel Feigheit, mit so viel raffinierter Brutalität, mit so viel Macht ausgefressen wurde. Ich habe in meinen Skizzen absichtlich keine Namen genannt, was kommt es auf Namen an! Der Feldwebel Nowotnik und der Leutnant Peters und der Hauptmann Dorbritz – wer kümmert sich denn hier um die! Um was hier gekämpft wird, das ist die Freiheit des Deutschen, das ist der unerschütterliche Glaube, daß es – auch beim Militär – keine Vorgesetzten außer Dienst gibt. »Disziplin ohne moralische Einsicht ist eine Absurdität«, hat Jakob Wassermann einmal gesagt. Nun, das deutsche Heer war absurd.

Schon regt sich allerorten die Erkenntnis, schüchtern keimen junge Knospen.

Im ›Tag‹ – man denke: im ›Tag‹! – erzählt am neunundzwanzigsten Januar Hauptmann z. D. Paschke vom Leben der höhern Stäbe im Felde, wie sie doch nicht immer so ein-

on the recruit—naturally on democratic principles. But now it is out turn.

We cannot expect a generation who could only live when—vain and puffed up—they endlessly overvalued and deified themselves, to take off the old sabre and become sensible and human. They are a lost cause. We want to deprive them of their subordinates. We do not want any more people to put up with that old lot and their artificially put on god-like countenances. We are free.

We were not free before. How despicable were the objections, how stuffy the most ridiculous objection of all: 'One must not generalize.' And yet generally everything was so generally mean . . .

Certainly these people cannot be reached by judicial means and court trials. When Rosa Luxemburg wrote of soldiers' abuses, they locked her up because they could not shine the light of the law on bestialities that had occurred in the cordoned-off barracks yards. And we will never be able to clearly prove that which was eroded with so much cowardice and refined brutality, with so much power. In my sketches, I have purposely named no names: what do names mean! Sergeant Nowotnik and Lieutenant Peters and Captain Dorbritz—who cares about them! What they are fighting for, is the German definition of freedom—the unshakeable faith that, even in the military, every superior is always on duty! Jakob Wassermann [the German-Jewish novelist] once said: 'Discipline without moral insight is an absurdity.' The German Army was therefore absurd.

Everywhere, this perception is growing, and new buds are opening.

In *Der Tag*—think of it—*Der Tag!* a report appeared on January 29, in which Captain Paschke describes the life of higher ranks in the field: how they really did not live

fach und bescheiden gelebt hätten, wie sie an sich und nur an sich auf Kosten der kämpfenden Truppe gedacht hätten; im ›Militärwochenblatt‹ berichtet in der Nummer 28 vom dreißigsten Januar ein General – er zeichnet K. –, wieviel unsaubere Elemente im deutschen Offizierkorps gewesen seien; in der ›Hilfe‹ spricht am sechzehnten Januar Miles – ein wegen seines Freimuts im Kriege verfolgter Offizier – von den Flecken, die die militärische Sonne verunzierten; in einer Flugschrift:›Warum erfolgte der Zusammenbruch an der Westfront?‹ registriert Otto Lehmann-Rußbüldt die Leiden und Qualen der gemeinen Soldaten; im Dezemberheft der ›Süddeutschen Monatshefte‹ gibt ein Oberarzt, der vierzig Monate an der Westfront gestanden hat, seine trüben Erlebnisse über die Verpflegung der Offiziere und die der Mannschaften zum besten. Dämmert es?

Es sind nicht nur ›Fälle‹ vorgekommen. Es sind beileibe nicht nur die Offiziere gewesen. Die Unteroffiziere habens nicht besser getrieben, der abkommandierte Mann nicht, wenn sie nur gekonnt haben.

Es war also nicht diese Schule der sittlichen Erziehung, von der die Fibeln und Schullesebücher und Reichstagsreden uns berichtet haben. Es war also nicht die Blüte der Nation, die da als Erzieher und Erzogene herumliefen: diese alten Unteroffiziere, die vom Leben außerhalb der Kaserne nur etwas Unterrock kannten, die aktiven Offiziere, die die Welt – auch die außerdeutsche – in ›Re'ment‹ und ›Zivil‹ einteilten, diese Reserve-Offiziere, die auf einmal zu fühlen begannen, wie doch auch sie zur Herrlichkeit geboren seien, und die ihr eigenes deutsches Nest beschmutzten, indem sie auf frühere Kollegen und Kameraden des Geistes traten.

Der lügt, der sagt, das müsse so sein. Man hat viel in der letzten Zeit um den Erlaß über die Kommandogewalt debattiert – man spricht von Neuordnung und vom deut-

as simply and modestly as they gave us to believe, but instead thought only of themselves, at the cost of the fighting troops. In the January 30 issue of *Militärwochenblatt* nr. 28, a General, called K, relates how many tainted elements there were in the German Officer Corps. In the January 16 issue of *Hilfe*, Miles—an officer persecuted during the war because of his candor—tells of the stain that spoiled the military sunshine. In a pamphlet *Why did the collapse on the Western Front occur,* Otto Lemann-Russbüldt registers the suffering and anguish of the ordinary soldier. In the December issue of the *Süddeutsche Monatshefte*, a senior physician who served on the Western Front for 40 months describes his gloomy experiences concerning the provisions of officers at the expense of the men. Does it finally dawn on you?

And these were not just isolated 'cases,' and certainly not limited to officers. Non-commissioned officers acted no better. nor men who were commandeered, if only they could do so.

It was therefore not this school of moral education, which school spelling and reading books and Reichstag speeches related to us. Nor was it the nation's finest flowes that milled around as the educators and the educated; these old non-commissioned officers, whose only knowledge of life outside the barracks was the world under the petticoat, the active officers who divided the world, in and inside Germany, into 'regimental' and 'civil: these reserve officers who suddenly began to feel how they too were born to glory, and who polluted their own German nest by treading on earlier colleagues and buddies.

The man who says that things must be this way is a liar. We have had many recent debates about the edict concerning Command authority—One speaks of a new order and

schen Volksheer. Hier hat eure Weisheit ein Ende, denn mit Verordnungen ist hier nichts getan.

»Aber wir brauchen das!« – »Aber es wird stets Offiziere geben!« Gewiß – nur, wenn die Deutschen wollen, nie mehr solche. Wer wehrt sich denn gegen sachliche Befehle und ihre Ausführung? Wer will denn nicht einem Führer folgen, wenn der nur einer ist? Deutschland baue sich eine Armee – aber in aller Zukunft wird keiner von uns bereit sein, sich von einem andern Deutschen – und trage er am Leibe allen Farbenschmuck eines Papageis – mit Füßen treten zu lassen; keiner wird andern als sachlichen Befehlen folgen, und jeder wird von dem Vorgesetzten verlangen, daß er die gleichen Mühen ertrage und den gleichen guten Willen zur Arbeit zeige wie der, von dem er sie fordert.

Mögen sich die Korps an der Ostgrenze zunächst ihre Satzungen nach eigenem Willen aufstellen. Das neue Heer, das mit jenen nichts gemein habe, sei die Schule des freien Mannes, eine lebende Einheit von Offizieren und Mannschaften. Ein Bruch mit der alten Armee–das sei die neue. Der lächerliche Grußerlaß ist kein froher Anfang. Der Offizier sei ein befehlender Kamerad. Das geht nicht? Dann lernts. Rücksichtslose Ausmerzung aller Früchte vom alten Stamm, gänzliche Abschaffung der alten Kommandogewalt, ein Wirbelwind fege die ›Herren‹ hinweg und setze Männer an ihre Stelle.

Und alle die Sprüche vom Vogel, der sein eigenes Nest beschmutzt, vom geschlagenen Riesen, der am Boden liegt, können uns nicht darüber hinwegtäuschen, daß das, was hier geschehen ist, eine schmerzhafte, aber heilsame Operation am deutschen Volkskörper gewesen ist. Es mußte gesagt werden, und es mußte jetzt gesagt werden. Die Gesinnung des deutschen Offiziers hat nichts getaugt, der Geist des deutschen Militärs hat nichts getaugt. Wir reißen sie aus unserm Herzen – wir spielen das Spiel nicht mehr mit.

Ein Scherbengericht? Anklage und Urteil?

a German militia army. Here, all your wisdom comes to an end because nothing is accomplished with orders.

'But we need this!' 'But there will always be officers!' Certainly—but, when the German people so wish, not those. Who fights against the implementation of objective orders? Who does not wish to follow a leader, if he is up to the task? Germany shall be building an army—but none of us will be ready in the future to be trodden underfoot by another German, even he wears all the colorful decorations of a parrot. Nobody will follow anything other than objective command, and each man will require from his superior that he takes the same trouble and has the same goodwill towards work as the man who is asked to do it.

The corps on our eastern border should initially establish their statutes according to their own will. The new army, which should have nothing in common with the old one, must be a school of free men, a living unit of officers and men. The laughable 'salute decree' is not a good beginning. The officer is a commanding buddy. That is not possible? Learn it now. Ruthless eradication of all the fruit of the old tree, complete abolition of the command structure, a whirlwind should sweep the old 'Sirs' away and place real men in their positions.

And all the sayings of birds who filthy their own nests, of defeated giants who lie prostrate, cannot hide the fact that what has happened here is a painful but salutary operation to the German nation's body. It must be said, and it must be said now. Neither the disposition of German officers nor the spirit of their army have been good for anything. We will tear them out of our hearts—we do not play their game anymore.

Exile courts? Accusation and judgment?

The primacy of army officers in German life is over.

Die Vorrangstellung des Offiziers im deutschen Leben ist dahin. Die viereinhalb Jahre sind dagewesen – darüber kommt kein Mann hinweg.

Es geht ja letzten Endes nicht um Paragraphen und Soldatenräte und um Verfügungen und Erlasse und Kompromisse und Vermittlungen. Es geht um die Wurst.

Wir Deutsche zerfallen in drei Klassen: die Untertanen – die haben bisher geherrscht; die Geistigen – die haben sich bisher beherrschen lassen; die Indifferenten – die haben gar nichts getan und sind an allem Elend schuld.

Und mit derselben Macht und mit derselben Faust wie die bunten Burschen, aber getrieben von strömendem Herzblut, ringen wir um die schlafenden Seelen Deutschlands. Land! es gibt Höheres, als vor der Geliebten mit einem Rang zu prunken! Land! wir Deutsche sind Brüder, und ein Knopf ist ein Knopf und ein Achselstück ein Achselstück. Kein Gott wohnt dahinter, keine himmlische Macht ist Menschen gegeben. Doch: eine. Die Menschen zu lieben, aber nicht, sie mit Füßen zu treten.

Wir speien auf das Militär – aber wir lieben die neue, uralte Menschlichkeit!

Prayer After the Slaughter

We have seen the last four and a half years—we cannot get away from that.

At the end of the day we are not talking about clauses and soldiers councils, regulations and decrees, compromises and arbitrations. We are talking everything: the nation itself.

There are three classes of Germans: subjects—they have reigned until recently; intellectuals—until recently they have allowed themselves to be ruled; the indifferent—they have done nothing at all and are guilty of all our misery.

And we are fighting, with the same power and the same fists as the colorful student associations, but driven by streaming heart's blood, for Germany's sleeping soul. Country! There is a higher goal than boasting to your mistress with a rank! Country! We Germans are brothers, but a button is a button and an epaulette an epaulette. No god lives behind them, people are given no heavenly power. Only one thing counts: To love one's fellow man, but not to stomp on them.

We spit on the military—But we love the new, age-old humanity!

Kurt Tucholsky

Kriegsgefangen

Kaspar Hauser, *Die Weltbühne,* 3. April 1919, wieder in: *Fromme Gesänge*

Wer hat in Belgiens Etappen regiert?
Offiziere! Offiziere!
Wer hat da im preußischen Ton kommandiert?
Offiziere! Offiziere!
Sollen die Belgier die Schuhe putzen:
Wir haben den Spaß, wir haben den Nutzen!
Aktiver Leutnant – kleiner Rat –
Einmal: Caesar! Wie wohl das tat!
„Wer nicht pariert, den stellt an die Wand!
(gezeichnet: Lehmann, Ortskommandant)."
Und die Belgier waren Menschen wie wir,
warteten ruhig der Jahre vier.
Bis sich der fremde Spuk entfernt.
Wen haben sie gründlich kenne gelernt?
Offiziere! Offiziere!

Kein Stroh auf dem Boden, kein Wasser, kein Bett,
es schlottern die dünnen Jacken.
„Mutter!" Wer jetzt einen Heimatgruß hätt!
Will der Tod uns noch nicht packen?
„Travailllez! En avant, les boches! Vite! Vite!"
ein Kolbenstoß in den Rücken.
Ein Mann, der vorbeifährt und das sieht,
muß die Tränen unterdrücken.
Wer frißt es aus, was für uns Vergangen?
Kriegsgefangen. Kriegsgefangen.

Prisoner of War

Kaspar Hauser, *Die Weltbühne,* April 3, 1919, again in: *Fromme Gesänge*

Who was in charge of Belgians in the rear?
The officers! The officers!
Who made their Prussian authority known?
The officers! The officers!
Time for the Belgians to polish our shoes:
We have some good fun, we get the job done!
Now Lieutenant—minor post –
Why not: Caesar! It felt so good!
"If they resist, up against the wall!
(signature: Lehmann, Town Commandant)."
And the Belgians were after all people like us,
biding their time while the four years went by
Until the foreign demon left.
And whom did they really get to know well?
The officers! The officers!

No straw on the floor there, no water, no bed,
the thin jackets shiver and shake.
"Mother!" If we just had some word from home!
Will Death not yet take us away?
"Travailllez! En avant, les boches! Vite! Vite!"
A rifle butt blow to the back.
Someone passing by who sees this take place
Must swallow the tears that would come.
Who pays for what we have done in the past?
The prisoners of war. The prisoners of war.

Wer frißt es aus, was scheinbar vorbei?
Die eigenen, unschuldigen Leute!
Deutschland, hörst du den Marterschrei?
Deutschland, tu es noch heute:
Stell die Burschen von damals vor ein Gericht!
Sie sind noch frei. Sie büßen ja nicht!
Sieh, wie sie wohl geborgen sitzen!
Mit ersparten Gehältern, mit Brüssler Spitzen –
Auge um Auge! Zahn um Zahn!
In die Hölle mit ihrem Caesarenwahn!
Deutschland, wo ist der Tag des Gerichts?
Deutschland, was tust du?
Nichts. Nichts. Nichts.

Prayer After the Slaughter

Who pays for the things some call over and done?
Our very own, innocent people!
Germans, hark to the martyr's cry.
Germans, do it today.
Seize those young rascals and take them to court.
They are still free. They make no amends.
See how well-taken care of they live!
With the money they saved and their fine lace from Brussels!
Eye for an eye and tooth for a tooth!
To hell with them and their Caesar complex!
Germany, what day is Judgment Day?
Germans, what do you say?
Nothing. Nothing. Nothing.

Austrian atrocities. Blindfolded and in a kneeling position, patriotic Serbians near the Austrian lines were arranged in a semi-circle and ruthlessly shot at a command.
Picture: Underwood & Underwood. (British War Dept.)

Kurt Tucholsky

Krieg dem Kriege

Theobald Tiger, *Der Ulk,* 13. Juni 1919

Sie lagen vier Jahre im Schützengraben.
Zeit, große Zeit!
Sie froren und waren verlaust und haben
Daheim eine Frau und zwei kleine Knaben,
weit, weit –!
Und keiner, der ihnen die Wahrheit sagt.
Und keiner, der aufzubegehren wagt.
Monat um Monat, Jahr um Jahr . . .

Und wenn mal einer auf Urlaub war,
sah er zu Haus die dicken Bäuche.
Und es fraßen dort um sich wie eine Seuche
Der Tanz, die Gier, das Schiebergeschäft.
Und die Horde alldeutscher Skribenten kläfft:
„Krieg! Krieg!
Großer Sieg!
Sieg in Albanien und Sieg in Flandern!"
Und es starben die andern, die andern, die andern . . .

Sie sahen die Kameraden fallen.
Das war das Schicksal bei fast allen:
Verwundung, Qual wie ein Tier, und Tod.
Ein kleiner Fleck, schmutzigrot –
Und man trug sie fort und scharrte sie ein.
Wer wird wohl der nächste sein?

Und ein Schrei von Millionen stieg auf zu den Sternen.
Werden die Menschen es niemals lernen?
Gibt es ein Ding, um das es sich lohnt?
Wer ist das, der do oben thront,

Make War on War

Theobald Tiger, *Der Ulk*, June 13, 1919

They lay in the trenches for four long years.
Time, a great time!
They froze, were lice ridden, and still had
At home a good wife and two little children,
Far, far away–!

And no one to tell them the truth of the war,
And no one who dared to stand up and protest.
Month after month, year after year . . .

And then when one of them went on leave,
At home he saw all the folks with fat bellies.
And all around he saw spread like the plague
The dancing, the greed, the black market profits.
And the horde of Pan German scribblers barks:
"War! War!
Victory galore!
A win in Albania, a win in Flanders!"
And the dying was done by the others, the others . . .

They saw their pals stagger and fall,
That was the fate of nearly them all.
Wounds, animal pain and then death.
A small spot, dirty-red –
And they carried them out and covered them up.
Who do you think will be next?

And a cry from the millions went up to the stars.
Will these people never learn?
Is there something that makes this worthwhile?
Who is it, sitting up there on the throne,

von oben bis unten bespickt mit Orden,
und nur immer befiehlt: Morden! Morden! –
Blut und zermalmte Knochen und Dreck ...
Und dann hieß es plötzlich, das Schiff sei leck.
Der Kapitän hat den Abschied genommen
Und ist etwas plötzlich von dannen geschwommen.
Ratlos stehen die Feldgrauen da.
Für wen das alles? Pro patria?

Brüder! Brüder! Schließt die Reihn!
Brüder! Das darf nicht wieder sein!
Geben sie uns den Vernichtungsfrieden,
ist das gleiche Los beschieden
unsern Söhnen und euren Enkeln.
Sollen die wieder blutrot besprenkeln
Die Ackergräben, das grüne Gras?
Brüder! Pfeift den Burschen was!
Es darf und soll so nicht weitergehn.
Wir habe alle, alle gesehn,
wohin ein solcher Wahnsinn führt –

Das Feuer brannte, das sie geschürt.
Löscht es aus! Die Imperialisten,
die da drüben bei jenen nisten
schenken uns wieder Nationalisten.
Und nach abermals zwanzig Jahren
Kommen neue Kanonen gefahren. –
Das wäre kein Friede.
Das wäre Wahn.
Der alte Tanz auf dem alten Vulkan.
Du sollst nicht töten! Hat einer gesagt.
Und die Menschheit hörts, und die Menschheit klagt.
Will das niemals anders werden?
Krieg dem Kriege!
Und Friede auf Erden.

Prayer After the Slaughter

Larded from top to bottom with medals
and whose only command is "Kill them! Kill them! –
Blood and ground-up bones and filth . . .
Then all of a sudden: "the ship's sprung a leak."
The captain has bidden us fond farewell
And was last seen swimming away.
The soldiers in grey now don't know what to do.
For whom was all this? Pro Patria?

Brothers! Brothers! Close the ranks!
Brothers, that must be the final time!
If ours is a Cartheginian peace,
The self same fate will soon befall
Our sons and your grandsons, too.
Shall they also sprinkle blood-red again
The trenches and the fresh green grass?
Brothers! Let them know what's up!
It must and cannot go on like this.
Every one of us has seen
Where such madness needs must lead –

The fire they fanned begins to burn.
Put it out! The imperialists
who make their nests with them over there
are producing a brood of nationalists here.
And in another twenty years,
New cannons for sure will be on their way. –
That would not be peace.
 That would be mad.
The same old dance on the same old volcano.
'Thou shall not kill' someone did say.
And humanity hears and humanity wails.
Can it never be otherwise?
Make war on war!
And peace on earth.

Kurt Tucholsky

Na, mein Sohn?

Ignaz Wrobel, *Die Weltbühne*, 3. Juli 1919

Besinnt ihr euch noch auf die Inspektionen eurer Truppenteile bei den Militärsoldaten? Wenn da die hohen und höhern und höchsten und allerhöchsten Offiziere durch die starren Reihen gingen und hier und da ein leutseliges Wort an die Kerls richteten? Erinnert ihr euch daran? »Na, mein Sohn, wo hast du dir denn das Eiserne Kreuz verdient?« Und der also Angeredete nahm die Nase noch steifer gradeaus und gab eine brave und leere Antwort, grade so dumm und leer wie die interesselose Frage, und der Inspizierende ging befriedigt weiter, und alles war gut . . .

War wirklich alles gut? War es die Aufgabe und der Lebenszweck der Führer, mit dieser falschen und gemachten Loyalität, die so viel Herablassung mit ebenso viel Menschenverachtung verband, zu dem niedern Volke herunterzusteigen? Es schien so. Denn sie hatten ja allesamt in diesem Kriege nicht begriffen, daß sie nicht mehr, wie in seligen Friedenszeiten, unter ihren Bauernjungens standen, unter denen der Leutnant so eine Art Gott war, weil er fließend lesen und schreiben konnte – (meist das einzige, was er konnte). Diesmal aber stak unter den grauen Kitteln ein gut Teil der Intelligenz des Landes, und wie hat es die berührt, wenn irgendein bunter Popanz ihnen leutselig und ganz von oben herunter die Frage stellte: »Na, mein Sohn?«

Wir verzichten auf diese Soldatenväter. Sie sind nicht ausgestorben. Es gibt immer noch viele unter den bürgerlichen ›Vorgesetzten‹, die annehmen, sie seien so etwas wie der alte Fritz und wir andern seien die braven potsdamer Rekruten,

Well, My Son?

Ignaz Wrobel, *Die Weltbühne,*
July 3, 1919

Do you still remember the military inspections of your military units? When the high, higher, highest, and all-highest officers walked through the rigid ranks, and here and there addressed an affable word to the fellows? Do you remember that? 'Well, my son, where did you earn this Iron Cross?' And the person addressed stuck his nose out straighter and gave a dutiful and empty answer, fully as dumb and empty as the uninterested question, and those inspecting moved forward satisfied, and all was good . . .

But was all really good? Was it the leaders' task and life's goal to descend from their lofty heights, with so much condescension and equally contempt for mankind, to the common people? It appears so. Because none of them grasped in this war, that the people they governed were not, like they have been in blissful peacetime, farmer's lads, for whom a lieutenant was a kind of God, because he could read and write fluently (even though this was mostly the only thing he knew). No, this time under the grey coats was a goodly part of the country's intelligentsia: and how did they feel when some colorful hobgoblin or other, affably and completely condescendingly, asked them: 'Well, my son?'

We can do without these pretend-fathers, but they have not died out. Many can still be found in the bourgeois 'superiors' who assume that they resemble Frederick the Great, and that we others are merely dutiful Potsdam re-

die sich stundenlang über ihren König unterhalten. Vorbei, vorbei –. Wir wollen Sachlichkeit im Betrieb und verzichten gut und gern auf diese kleinen menschlichen Kniffe.

Die Deutschen sind noch lange nicht dazu erzogen, miteinander zu arbeiten. Sie können nur wirken, wenn man sie einen über den andern stellt. Das kommt uns zum Halse heraus. Zusammenarbeiten! ist die Losung, nicht: Unterstellen! Hand in Hand arbeiten heißt es, nicht: Überordnen. Damit ist gar nichts geschafft; das nutzt nichts, sondern schadet nur: diese Kompetenzstreitigkeiten, dieses Raufen, wer nun mehr zu sagen hat, und wer am allermeisten zu sagen hat. Das führt uns nicht weiter, sondern treibt nur von der Arbeit ab. Und vielleicht erleben wir doch noch einmal die Zeit, wo sich kein Deutscher mehr zu dem eigenen Landsmann leutselig und ohne innere Anteilnahme herabläßt, und ihm gutmütig auf die Schulter klopft und kopfnickend zu fragen geruht: »Na, mein Sohn?«

cruits who chatter for hours about their king. This period is over, over—we want business objectivity and completely renounce these small human gimmicks.

The German people have not been educated to work with each other for long. They can only work when one is put over the other. We are sick and tired of it. 'Work together!' is the solution, not subordinate! It means to work hand in hand, not place over. Nothing is achieved by this, it helps nobody. Rather it damages: this responsibility conflict, fighting with each other about who has more, and who has most, to say. It gets us nowhere, only drives us away from work. And perhaps we will still witness the time, when no German will condescend affably and without inner participation to a countryman, clap him good-naturedly on the shoulder, and head nodding, ask: 'Well, my son?'

Kurt Tucholsky

S'ist Krieg

Kaspar Hauser, *Die Weltbühne*, 31. Juli 1919

Die fetten Hände behaglich verschränkt
Vorn über der bauchigen Weste,
steht Einer am Lager und lächelt und denkt:
„'s ist Krieg! Das ist doch das Beste!
Das Leder geräumt, und der Friede ist weit.
Jetzt mach ich in andern Chosen –

Noch ist die blühende, goldene Zeit!
Noch sind die Tage der Rosen!"

Franz von der Vaterlandspartei
Klatscht Bravo zu donnernden Reden.
Ein ganzer Held – stets ist er dabei,
wenn sich Sprecher im Sale befehden.
Die Bezüge vom Staat, die Nahrung all right
Laß Stürme donnern und tosen –
Noch ist die blühende, goldene Zeit!
Noch sind die Tage der Rosen!

Tage der Rosen! Regierte sich je
So leicht und bequem wie heute?
Wir haben das Prae und das Portepee[*]
Und beherrschen geduckte Leute.
Wir denken an Frieden voll Ängstlichkeit
Mit leider gefüllten Hosen –

Noch . . . Noch ist die goldene, die blühende Zeit!
Noch sind die Tage der Rosen!

---

[*] Having Prae indicates that one enjoys privileges conferred by superior rank in the Wilhelmenian society. Porteepee was uniform trim used to distinguish a superior officer.

It's War

Kaspar Hauser, *Die Weltbühne*, July 31, 1919

His fat hands most comfortably folded and laced
In front of his baggy old waistcoat,
He stands at his warehouse and smiles as he thinks:
"This war! It's the best thing for business!
The leather is gone and there's no peace in sight.
It's time to switch gears and get going –

We are still living in our golden years!
We are still gathering roses!"

Franz from the Fatherlands Party
Claps Bravo to thundering speeches.
A real hero, he—he is always on hand
When speakers in chambers start fighting.
The state subsidies, the nutrition, all right.
Let the storms thunder and roar.
We are still living in our golden years!
We are still gathering roses!

Day of the roses! Since when has it been
So easy to govern as now?
We can pull rank and our sword knots are tight
And we rule over cowering people.
But we think of peace with fear and dread
And, sadly, a load in our pants—

Yet . . . We are still living in our golden years!
We are still gathering roses!

This poem was banned during World War I

Nach fünf Jahren

Kaspar Hauser, *Die Weltbühne,* 7. August 1919

Und Vater tot und Bruder tot
und einer kriegsgefangen;
und Mutter sitzt in Rentennot:
Was essen meine Rangen . . . ?
So stehn wir da im schäbigen Kleid
und denken an die alte Zeit.
Und hassen.

Und hassen jenen Preußengeist,
der uns geduckt, betrogen.
Und hassen, was von Orden gleißt.
Ihr Aar ist fortgeflogen.
Er hinterließ als armen Rest
uns nur ein ganz beschmutztes Nest
und graue Elendsmassen.
Wir hassen.

Hör, Bruder, standest du nicht stramm
vor Knechten und vor Schiebern?
Du gingst zur Schlacht als Opferlamm.
Wir fiebern, fiebern, fiebern . . .
Wach auf! Du warst so lange krank!
Es dauert nicht ein Leben lang!
Mußts nur nicht gehen lassen!
Wir hassen.

Five Years Later

Kaspar Hauser, *Die Weltbühne*, August 7, 1919

And father dead and brother dead
Another lies in prison,
And mother cannot pay the rent
What will I feed the children?
We stand around in shabby clothes
 And think about the good old days,
And hate!

We hate the same old Prussian ways
That have deceived and cheated,
We hate their shining medals too
Their eagle's flown, departed;
And left us with its sad remains,
A dirty and polluted nest,
And poor grey hordes of beggars.
We hate!

Hear, brothers, didn't you stand up straight
for traffickers and toadies?
You went to slaughter like a lamb.
We simmer, simmer, simmer . . .
Awake! For so long you've been sick,
It will not last your whole life long!
You can't just let things go!
We hate!

Brenn aus! Brenn aus! Mit Stumpf und Stiel!
Greif mutig in den Himmel!
Die Oberschicht – sie zählt nicht viel –
versinkt in dem Gewimmel.
In Dreck und Blut und Schlamm und Schmerz
blieb uns ein warmes Menschenherz.
Schlag zu mit wuchtigen Hieben!
Wir lieben!

Burn out, burn out both root and branch.
Reach to the sky with courage!
The upper class—they don't mean much –
sinks back into the masses.
In filth and blood and mud and pain,
a feeling human heart remains.
Lash out with mighty blows!
We love!

British 55th (West Lancashire) division troops blinded by tear gas await treatment at an Advanced Dressing Station near Bethune during the Battle of Estaires, April 10, 1918, part of the German offensive in Flanders.
Picture: Imperial War Museum, London

Kurt Tucholsky

Zwei Mann: Gitarre und Mandoline

Ignaz Wrobel, *Berliner Volkszeitung*,
14. August 1919

Im Waldlager 1917. Der Major steht vor dem Bataillonsunterstand und spiegelt sich in der Sonne. Wir stehen im Stellungskrieg, seit langen Monaten im Stellungskrieg, und jetzt ist August, der Feind ist ruhig, die Marketenderei klappt, die Herren trinken abends ihren Sekt und denken sich am Tage immer etwas Neues aus, um das Leben ein bißchen abwechslungsreicher zu machen. Birkengeländer um die Offiziersunterstände haben wir schon. Es werden zwar die feindlichen Flieger auf uns aufmerksam werden, aber dafür sieht es schön aus. Schön wie eine Ansichtskarte. Schilder an allen Ecken und Kanten haben wir auch. Die Offiziersunterstände sind pompös ausgebaut. Wir haben alles, Verzeihung, die Herren haben alles.

Und nun steht der feiste Kommandeur in der Sonne und glänzt und strahlt und denkt nach, was man jetzt aufführen könnte. Richtig! – »Waren da nicht neulich zwei Kerls, die Musik machen konnten? Jeije oder so was?« – Der Adjutant wippt nach vorn. »Gewiß, Herr Major! Sehr wohl, Herr Major! Zwei Mann aus der dritten Kompanie. Einer spielt Gitarre, der andere Mandoline. Hört sich sehr hübsch an. Vielleicht könnten die heute abend, wenn ich mir den Vorschlag erlauben darf . . . ?« – »Kerls sollen heute abend antreten. Um neun Uhr. Kriegen Freibier.«

Und sie treten an, und die kleinen Lampions schaukeln im Winde, das Kasino hat in der Birkenlaube decken las-

Two Men: Guitar and Mandolin

Ignaz Wrobel, *Berliner Volkszeitung,*
August 14, 1919

In a forest camp, 1917. The major stands in front of the battalion trench, reflected in the sun. We are in the midst of static warfare, and have been for months. And now it is August 1, the enemy is quiet, the suttleries are running smoothly. In the evening, our honored gentlemen drink their champagne, and always think of something new during the day, to make our lives somewhat more varied. We already have birch railing around the officer's trenches. This will draw the enemy fliers' attention to us, but it already looks like a picture postcard. We also have signs in every corner and edge. The officer's trenches have been constructed splendidly and pompously. We have everything: excuse me, the gentlemen have everything.

And now the plump commander stands in the sun, shines and beams, and reflects on what must be done today—Right! –'Were there not recently two chaps here who could make music? Jeije or something?'—The adjutant bobs forward. 'Certainly, Herr Major! Very well, Herr Major! Two men from Third Company. One plays guitar, the other mandolin. It sounds quite charming. Perhaps we can this evening, if I may allow myself to suggest . . .?' 'The fellows must report this evening at 9.00 pm. They will receive free beer.'

And they report and the small lanterns sway in the wind. The officer's mess in the birch grove has set its

sen, und es gibt schöne Sachen, die so ein Musketier noch nie im Kriege zu sehen bekommen hat: Gänseleberpastete und Gurken und kalten Fisch und Rotwein und Sekt und Weißwein und viele, viele Schnäpse . . . Die Spieler stehen schüchtern am Eingang der Laube. Dem einen schluckts im Halse – seine Frau schreibt, sie stehe täglich zwei Stunden nach Kartoffeln an . . . . . »Na, spielt mal was, ihr beiden!« ruft der Major gutgelaunt herüber. Und sie fassen ihre Instrumente fester, verständigen sich durch einen Blick, und durch die lauten und lustigen Gespräche der Offiziere zimpert es – drohend? warnend? – klar und melodisch: »In der Heimat – in der Heimat – da gibts ein Wiedersehn . . . «

Staubiger Stadtsommer 1919. Am Ausgang eines berliner Stadtbahnhofs stehen zwei Mann, krüppelig und zerlumpt: Gitarre und Mandoline. Jedesmal, wenn die Fahrgäste eines Zuges auf die Straße herunterströmen, fassen die beiden ihre Instrumente fester, verständigen sich durch einen Blick, und los gehts: »In der Heimat – in der Heimat – da gibts ein Wiedersehn . . . «

Wo habe ich die beiden Grauen nur schon einmal gesehn? –

tables with such wonderful things no musketeer has yet seen in this war. Goose liver paté, pickles, cold fish; red wine, champagne, white wine, and schnapps: a great deal of schnapps. The players stand timidly at the entrance of the bower. One man gulps—his wife wrote that she has to stand in line for 2 hours for potatoes. 'So, play something, both of you!' calls the major good-naturedly. And they grasp their instruments more tightly, communicate with a look, and the music whimpers through the officers' loud, jolly conversation—threatening? Warning?—Clear and melodic. 'At home—at home—we will see each other there again . . .'

Dusty summer in the city, 1919. Two men stand at the entrance of a Berlin city train station, crippled and in rags. Guitar and mandolin. Each time the train passengers stream out from train to street, the two grasp their instruments more tightly, communicate with a look, and it starts; 'At home—at home—we will see each other there again.'

Where have I seen these two boys in grey before?—

Kurt Tucholsky

Der Krieg ohne Namen

Ignaz Wrobel, *Berliner Tageblatt*
17. August 1919

Frühere große Zeiten hatten so schöne Namen, die wir schwitzend in der Schule lernen mußten. Da gab es einen Siebenjährigen Krieg, und einen Kartoffelkrieg, und einen Bayerischen Erbfolgekrieg – wer dessen Vorgeschichte aufsagen konnte, war bei unserm Geschichtslehrer, dem Rotbart, fein heraus – und einen Spanischen Erbfolgekrieg und einen Freiheitskrieg – und viele schöne andre.

Aber wie heißt nun dieser? Ich muß ›dieser‹ sagen – denn er hat noch keinen Namen. Ich weiß ja nun nicht, ob die andern schönen Kriege ihren glorreichen Namen gleich angehängt bekommen haben, während sie noch geführt wurden – bei dem dreißigjährigen ist das zum Beispiel zweifelhaft – aber ›dieser‹ hat noch keinen. Bekommt er mal einen?

Vorläufig irrt er noch, blutig und übel, durch das Gedächtnis der Lebenden, und er hat so wenig einen Namen, wie die Sonne einen besondern Vornamen führt. Es gibt nur die eine. Und es gibt nur den einen. ›Der Krieg‹ sagen die Leute. Und man weiß schon . . .

»Und dann habe ich im Kriege . . . « – »Dann kam der Krieg.« (Berühmter Satz in Novellen.) – »Während des Krieges ist dann . . . . .« – Und jeder weiß merkwürdigerweise genau, welcher Krieg gemeint ist, und denkt gar nicht an den Spanischen Erbfolgekrieg und an den zweiten Türkenkrieg – sondern nur an den einen, an diesen einen . . .

Aber kann das so weiter gehen? Wird dieser Krieg nicht auch einmal einen Namen bekommen? Wie werden ihn unsere Enkel lernen?

The War Without Name

Ignaz Wrobel, *Berliner Tageblatt,* August 17, 1919

Previous grandiose periods had such beautiful names that we had to learn in school, sweating at our desks. There was a Seven Years War, a Potato War, a Bavarian War of Succession—whoever knew why that one happened got extra points with our red-bearded history teacher—, a Spanish War of Succession, a War of Liberation, and many lovely other names.

But what do we call this war? I must say 'this,' because it is still nameless. I don't know whether the previous lovely wars got their glorious names attached while they were still being waged: it is doubtful with the Thirty Years War, for example. But 'this' one has no name yet: will it acquire one?

For the moment it is still wandering, bloody and beastly, through the memory of the living. Like the sun has no first name, it has no name either. There is only one sun, and likewise there is only one war. We call it 'The War,' and know exactly what we mean.

'And then in the war I . . .' 'Then came the war' (a famous phrase in novels), 'then, during the war . . .' And, strangely enough, everyone knows exactly which war is being referred to, and doesn't think of the War of Spanish Succession and the Second Turkish War—but of the other, this one war . . .

But can it continue like this? Won't this war also, at some point, acquire a name? How will our grandchildren learn about it?

Als ›Weltkrieg‹? – Da habe ich Bedenken. Denn die Propheten, die vom Prophezeien und von den Kriegen leben, weissagen uns einen baldigen schrecklichen Krieg zwischen Amerika und Japan, und ob das nicht auch eine Art Weltkrieg werden wird, steht noch sehr dahin. Also wie denn?

Also wie denn?

Ich schlage vor, wir einigen uns auf das Etikett, das man den vier Jahren angehängt hat, als man noch reklamiert und im Vollbesitze der heimischen Butter war. Als alles noch so glatt war und so einfach: die einen starben, und die anderen machten Haßgesänge. Die einen verkamen im Dreck, und die anderen lobpriesen das . . .

Einigen wir uns, wenn wir von diesen Jahren und von diesem Kriege sprechen, freundlich und mit fast unmerklicher Ironie das Ding so zu benamsen, wie man es damals nannte, als noch die Oberste Heeresleitung täglich ihren Kleinen Katechismus drucken ließ:

Die große Zeit.

'World War?' I have misgivings about this name—Prophets, who live from prophecy and war, predict an imminent and terrible war between the United States and Japan. Whether this will be a type of World War as well, remains to be seen. And so?

And so?

I suggest that we agree on the label attached to these four years, when we still complained, and did not have to stand in line for butter. When everything was so easy and so simple. One person died, the other composed hymns of hate. One decayed in filth, the other sang songs of praise to that . . .

Let us agree that, when we speak of these years, and of this war, we'll call that thing, cordially and with nearly imperceptible irony, as it was called when Supreme Army Command still used to print their daily Shorter Catechism:

The Great Time.

Kurt Tucholsky

Das erdolchte Heer

Von einem Berliner, *Berliner Volkszeitung*, 23. November 1919

Die Generale habens gesagt
Und haben die Heimat angeklagt.

Die Heimat – heißt es – erdolchte das Heer.
Aber die Heimat litt viel zu sehr!

Sie schrie und ächzte unter der Faust.
Es würgt der Hunger, der Winterwind saust.

Ihr habt der Heimat erst alles genommen
Und seid noch besiegt zurückgekommen.

Besiegt hat euch euer eigener Wahn.
Dreimal kräht jetzt der biblische Hahn.

Und nach soviel Fehlern und falschen Taten:
Habt ihr nun auch die Heimat verraten.

Die Heimat, die Frauen, die Schwachen, die Kranken –
Wir danken, Generale, wir danken!

The Backstabbed Army

By a Berliner, *Berliner Volkszeitung*, November 23, 1919

The generals have spoken up
And accused the homeland of selling out.

The homeland—they say—put a knife in the troops.
But the homeland has suffered much too much!

It shrieked in agony under the fist.
Ground down by hunger: the winter wind howled.

You first took away everything that we had
And then returned beaten in spite of it all.

Your arrogant vanity caused you to fail.
Thrice now he crows, the Biblical cock.

And after your blunders and deeds false to tell,
You now have betrayed your homeland as well.

The homeland, the women, the weak, sick and such -
Say thank you, generals, thank you so much!

Kurt Tucholsky

Ich habe noch . . .

Peter Panter, *Berliner Tageblatt*, 24. November 1919

»Ich habe noch meinen alten Paletot« – auf diesem traurig merkwürdigen Satz beruhen heute unendlich viele Existenzen. Sie haben noch . . . Die alten Dinge aus dem Frieden, die Anzüge, die Kragen, die Möbel und die Teppiche – Dinge, die während des Krieges still auf ihren Herrn gewartet haben, und nun sind sie noch da. Noch . . . Wie lange noch . . . ?

Eine ganze Schicht lebt heute das alte Leben weiter fort, aber es ist ein Scheinleben; das Rad läuft, aber der Antrieb ist gehemmt. Noch läuft es. Eine ganze Schicht fragt sich jeden Morgen besorgt und beschwert, wie lange es noch so wird weitergehen können. Denn die alten Sachen, die noch vorhanden sind, das Material, das heftig in Anspruch genommen wird: es wird eines Tages verbraucht sein, es muß erneuert werden, aber das kostet Geld, es wird also nicht erneuert werden – nun gut, und dann –?

Dann wird eine Schicht, die heute nicht das schlechteste am Mittelstand darstellt, untergegangen sein, leise, klanglos, still, ohne daß es einer merken wird. Untergehen – die Menschen gehen nicht unter. Sie verelenden. Und das geschieht ohne viel Lärm und Aufsehen.

Aber wird es keiner merken? Wir merkens schon. Wir merken, daß jener feine, unwägbare Einfluß fehlt, der von diesen Leuten, die da heute am Verelenden sind, immer ausgegangen ist. Die Lauten treten an ihre Stelle, die Robusten, jene, die zu jeder Konzession bereit sind, und die Geld verdienen, haben, scheffeln. Und so geht unser Bestes langsam vor die Hunde.

I still have . . .

Peter Panter, *Berliner Tageblatt*, November 24, 1919

"I still have my old German greatcoat"—An endless number of lives today are based upon that sad and strange sentence. They still have . . . their old peacetime things: the suits, collars, furniture, carpets—things that, during wartime, quietly waited for their owner, and now they are still here . . . But for how long?...

An entire stratum of society continues to live the good old life, but it is a sham; the wheel turns, but the propulsion is obstructed. It still works. An entire layer of society asks every morning, anxious and aggrieved, how long it can continue like this: The old things they still have, the material that is frequently used—one day it will be used up and will have to be renewed. But this costs money, so it will therefore not be renewed. Well, but what will happen then--?

Then a social stratum that today represents a reasonable middle class will have perished: silent, noiseless, quiet, without anyone noticing it. Perish? The people do not perish, they become pauperized. And this happens without much noise or sensation.

But will nobody really notice? We see it already. We see the lack of that subtle, imponderable influence that always originated from these people, who are today the most pauperized. Rowdy people fill their shoes—resilient people who are ready to make every concession and have raked the money in. And so our best and brightest slowly go down the drain.

Es geht langsam. Im Kriege wurden diese Dinge humoristisch genommen – man lachte, weil dies oder jenes so rar oder so teuer war und wurde, daß man es sich nicht zulegen konnte – aber das ist der Krieg, nicht wahr, und er wird vorbeigehen ... Aber er ging nicht vorbei, er ist bis heute nicht vorbeigegangen, und die Dinge, die über den Etat gehen, werden immer zahlreicher, und die kleinen, nagenden Sorgen werden immer mehr und mehr ... Es geht langsam. Es fing mit einer ganz unbedeutenden Qualitätsminderung im Handschuhkauf an und bei den Stiefeln; es begann damit, daß man zufrieden war, überhaupt Butter zu bekommen, deren Beschaffenheit längst nicht mehr zur Diskussion stand, es begann damit, daß man dies und jenes unterließ, dieses oder jenes liebe Buch nicht kaufte und der gnädigen Frau ein paar Rosen weniger zu schicken in der Lage war ... Es ging langsam.

Bis das Tempo lebhafter wurde. Bis aus den kleinen Unbequemlichkeiten große Unannehmlichkeiten, und aus diesen nackte Sorgen wurden. Bis eine ganze Schicht in diesem Lande erkannte: Ruin! So geht das nicht weiter! Und bis aus einem bescheidenen Mittelstand etwas wird, das noch immer der Tod allen geistigen Lebens gewesen ist: wirtschaftliches Proletariat. Ehre dem Proletarier, der trotz der Mietkaserne Bücher liest! Ehre dem jungen Arbeiter, der sich fortbildet, und der es zu etwas bringt! Helden. Und Ausnahmen. Wer kann das –?

All die kleinen Lehrerinnen, die Beamten, die kaufmännischen Angestellten und ihre Angehörigen – diese ganze Schicht, die bis dahin den empfänglichsten Boden für die Gaben der Künstler gebildet hatte, die so dankbar waren für alles, was ihnen gegeben wurde – sie sind in der Nähe des Untergangs. Heute haben sie noch. Und dann –?

Unsere Väter sind alt und sitzen in ihren Möbeln. Unsere Kinder werden vielleicht einmal wieder in der Lage sein, sich in die ihren zu setzen. Aber wir? Aber die Dazwi-

Prayer After the Slaughter

Things happen slowly. During wartime they have their humorous aspects—one laughed because this or that was so scarce, or so expensive that it couldn't be acquired at all.—But that is war, isn't it, and it will be over . . . But it did not go away, and still has not gone away. And the items that are over our budget become ever more numerous, and the small, gnawing cares are always increasing and increasing . . . Things happen slowly. It started with a wholly insignificant quality reduction in the purchase of gloves and boots. It started with the fact that one was satisfied to obtain butter—whose quality had long since ceased to be a topic of discussion—at all. It started when we did without this or that, did not buy this or that good book, and we had to send the hostess a few less roses . . . It happened slowly.

Until the pace started to pick up. Until small inconveniences became large unpleasantnesses, and then naked anxieties. Until one stratum of society in this country recognized only ruin! It cannot go one like this! Until the modest middle class changes into something that has always been the death of all spiritual life: economic proletariat. Honor the proletariat, who reads books despite living in a tenement! Honor the young worker, who educates himself and achieves something! Heroes. And exceptions. Who can do that --?

All the modest (female) teachers, government employees, white-collar workers and their families—this entire layer who until now has formed the most receptive soil for artistic talents, and were so thankful for everything that was given them—they are all near extinction. Today they still have something. But after that -?

Our fathers are old and sit in their armchairs. Our children may perhaps again be in a position to sit in theirs. But we? Those who live in between these gen-

schenlebenden? Es besteht gar kein Zweifel, daß es heute für den Mann des Mittelstandes eine blanke Unmöglichkeit ist, eine Frau heimzuführen, die nicht im Besitz großer Geldmittel ist. Es besteht gar kein Zweifel, daß diese Lage nicht nur wirtschaftlich von den schwersten Folgen begleitet sein wird, sondern vor allem geistig. Wohin treiben wir? Wohin werden wir getrieben?

Noch geht im großen und ganzen das Spiel mit den alten Kulissen weiter. Noch wird verlangt, daß jeder reine und gut gepflegte Leibwäsche trägt – und er kann das ja auch, weil er sie noch besitzt. Aber wenn sie abgenutzt ist, was dann –? Noch täuscht man sich selbst mühsam vor, es habe sich ja im großen und ganzen nichts gewandelt, und es sei gewiß eine schwere Zeit, aber man werde wohl immerhin ... Nun sind aber wirtschaftliche Gesetze stark, sehr stark – und ich sehe über das Land: angestrengt, die Lippen zusammengekniffen, mit gefurchter Stirn, stemmen sich Tausende und Tausende gegen das Rad des großen Wagens, der unaufhaltsam seinen Weg zu machen gesonnen ist, sie ächzen, die beste Manneskraft geht dahin – aber der Wagen rollt.

Der Typus des stillen Helden, den Thomas Mann für die deutsche Literatur entdeckt hat – er ist nie größer gewesen als in dieser Zeit. Nicht nur, daß die feinsten Köpfe gezwungen sind, für Geld Dinge herzustellen, die mit ihrem innersten Wesen nichts zu tun haben – wieviel Energie gehört dazu, wieviel Zähigkeit, wieviel Glaube!

Denn noch glauben sie. Die Schuhe sind nicht mehr sehr gut, die Anzüge bieten das Bild jenes leisen und schrecklichen Verfalls, das nur ein Frauenauge zu sehen in der Lage ist, die Möbel sind in ihren Ersatzteilen nicht mehr harmonisch – es geht langsam, ganz langsam bergab. Aber der Glaube blieb.

Noch glauben sie alle. Noch glauben sie, es könne damit nicht abgetan sein. Es könne so nicht aufhören. Dafür könnte die Generation ihrer Väter und Vorväter nicht

erations? There is no doubt at all that it is completely impossible for a middle class man to bring home a wife, except she possesses a lot of money herself. There is also no doubt that this situation will have the direst consequences, not only in economic terms, but even more primarily spiritual. Where are we drifting? Where are we being driven?

Now, all things considered, the play continues with the old backdrop. Everyone is still required to wear clean skivvies—and he can, because he still has them. But when they wear out, what then --? We still laboriously delude ourselves that in principle nothing has changed: Times are certainly hard, but we will, after all . . . Economic laws are strict, very strict—I see across the land strain: strain, pursed lips, furrowed brows. Thousands upon thousands brace themselves against the wheel of the great wagon which inexorably wants to move. They groan, their best manpower goes into the effort—but the wagon rolls.

The character of the quiet hero, which Thomas Mann has discovered for German literature, has never been greater than in our own time. It is not only that money compels our best minds to manufacture things which have nothing to do with their innermost being—how much energy, how much tenacity and faith!

Because they still believe. Their shoes aren't as good any more, their suits show evidence of that slow but terrible decay that only a woman's eye can see. Their furniture replacement parts do not fit any more—things are going downhill slowly, so very slowly. But they still believe.

They all still believe. They still believe that it cannot be dismissed, cannot cease. The generation of their fathers and forefathers could not have fought so hard just for this ('My son should have it better than I!'). They still believe.

gerungen haben (»Mein Junge soll mal was Besseres werden!«) – noch glauben sie. Und ich weiß zwar nicht, ob die Nationalökonomen, die restlos alles nach ökonomischen Gesetzen erklären wollen, lächeln werden: aber ich denke, daß dieser Glaube stärker ist als wirtschaftliche Gesetze.

Laßt nicht ab! Bleibt diesem Glauben treu! Es ist euer Bestes. Wir alle sehen, wie es bergab geht, unaufhaltsam bergab, und wie wenig Hoffnung ist, daß wir jemals die Zeiten des billigen Inselbuches (das mir geradezu als Symptom dieser Schicht erscheint), wieder erleben werden. Glaubt dennoch! Ihr seid nicht allein.

Die unerbittliche Mühle des Tages klappert. Tagaus, tagein. Leuchtendes Jugendland versinkt – das, was wir geliebt haben, ist Luxus geworden, heute fast ausnahmslos in den Händen derer, die es sich mit Geld erkaufen wollen – aber das geht nicht, geht zum Glück nicht. Wir hatten gehofft, es später, in besseren Zeiten, wiederzuerlangen – dafür haben wir gearbeitet, dafür durchgehalten. Was der beneidenswert robustere Teil der Bevölkerung nicht merkt: wir haben es empfunden. Und wollten es bewahren. Und nun laufen die Tage, rinnen dahin -und was bleibt uns? Noch geht es, noch können wir – noch einen Arbeitsmonat, noch dies, noch das – gewiß, noch geht es. Aber wie lange? Und besser werden wir nicht dabei.

Glaubt, glaubt. Haltet fest, ihr kleinen Kaufleute, und ihr, Lehrer, haltet fest, Angestellte und Arbeiter und Handwerker! Haltet fest. Die Valuta ist gefallen, diese Valuta darf nicht sinken. Ihr tragt sie in euern Händen. Und haltet fest, ihr Mädchen, die ihr das Kostbarste im Herzen habt, das es für die gibt, die euch lieben. Und halt auch du fest, liebste Frau – und warte. Warten ist schließlich das Schönste auf der Welt.

»Wir haben noch . . .« Nicht lange mehr, und ein härterer Kampf wird beginnen, als der war, der um jenes Fort

And I do not know whether the national economists, who want to explain everything solely by economic laws, will laugh, but I think that this faith is stronger than their economic rules.

Do not stop! Remain true to this faith! It is your best chance. We all see how things are going downhill, inexorably downhill, and how little hope there is that we will ever witness the times of the cheap book from Inselverlag (which really seems to me to be the hallmark of this social stratum) again. But still, have faith! You are not alone.

The day's inexorable mill clatters. Day in, day out. The shining land of our youth sinks away.—That which we loved has become a luxury and is today, almost without exception, in the hands of those who want to buy everything off with money—but luckily it doesn't work that way. We have hoped to acquire these again later during better times—we have worked for that, we have persevered for that. What the enviably robust portion of the population does not notice, is that we have felt it.—And we want to preserve it. And now the days pass and run away—and what remains for us? It still works, we are still able—just another month of work, just this, just that -- surely it is still working. But for how long? And things do not improve.

Have faith, faith, you small merchants, and teachers, have faith! Officials, workers and artisans! Hold fast. The currency has fallen, but this currency cannot fall. You hold it in your own hands. And young girls, hold fast to the most valuable thing that exists, the feeling in your hearts, that there are those who love you. Hold fast, dear lady—and wait. To wait is at the end of the day the most beautiful thing in the world.

'We still have.' In a short time, a battle will begin that is harder and more fateful than the one which raged over

Douaumont tobte. Und ein schicksalsreicherer. Trösten kann niemand. Aber anfeuern und ausharren machen. Und an eins der schönsten Worte Christian Morgensterns erinnern:

> Dulde. Trage.
> Bessere Tage
> werden kommen.
> Alles muß frommen,
> denen, die fest sind.
> Herz, altes Kind,
> dulde, trage!

Es wird – scheltet mich nicht einen Metaphysiker – doch einmal belohnt werden.

Fort Douaumont in Verdun. No one can comfort you. But what they can do is to encourage you up, make you stay the course, and remind you of some of Christian Morgenstern's most beautiful words:

> Be patient, bear up/
> Better days/
> Will come/
> All things must benefit/
> Those who hold fast/
> Take heart, old child/
> Be patient, bear up.

Do not deride me as a metaphysicist—one day we will be rewarded.

German war cinema crew on the Western Front in the trenches working to document the war, also for propaganda purposes. Picture: Deutsches Bundesarchiv, Kriegskinematographie

Kurt Tucholsky

Der Mantel

Ignatz Wrobel, *Berliner Volkszeitung*,
14. Dezember 1919

Gegenüber von mir, in der Elektrischen Bahn, sitzt eine Frau mit einem dicken, feldgrauen Mantel. Das Tuch ist an manchen Stellen merkwürdig dunkel, an manchen heller – es ist kein sehr feiner Mantel mehr. Und wie sie da so sitzt, muß ich auf einmal daran denken, was dieser Mantel schon alles gesehen hat.

Lieber, alter Mantel! Wo bist du überall gewesen? In Flandern hat er dich getragen, durch Lehm und Dreck, in grauen Regentagen und in den langen, dunkeln Nächten, wenn er Posten schob – in Polen vielleicht und in Rumänien. Du tratest mit dem Stück Mensch, das da in dich eingewickelt war, zum Appell an, und du marschiertest in Reih und Glied mit tausend anderen Mänteln an Seiner Majestät vorüber, und der freute sich, wie viele Mäntel doch seine Armee hätte. Die Menschen sah er nicht ... Du wurdest gebürstet und geklopft, und wie ein Anhängsel begleitete dich in deinen Feldzügen ein kleines, unglückseliges Menschenkind, das sich so nach Hause sehnte und nach Ruhe, und das endlich, endlich wieder bei Muttern sitzen wollte. Was da in dich eingewickelt war, Mantel, das war nicht faul und nicht träge, und die Front hat es auch nicht erdolcht. Aber es war ein Mensch ...

Du hattest es gut, lieber Mantel. Du fühltest nichts, warst also gewissermaßen das Ideal eines Soldaten. Und es kam ja auch schließlich, wenn man es recht bedenkt, bei dieser Armee viel mehr auf den Mantel an, als auf das, was drinnen war. In der Kammer wurdet ihr Mäntel gepflegt und gehegt und ausgezählt und sorgsam behütet. Die Men-

The Coat

Ignatz Wrobel, *Berliner Volkszeitung,* December 14, 1919

Opposite me in the electric streetcar sits a woman with a thick, field grey coat. The cloth is peculiarly dark in some places, lighter in others—no, it isn't a very fine coat any more. And the way she sits there, I suddenly have to think about everything that this coat has seen already.

Dear old coat! How many places have you been in? He wore you in Flanders, through mud and filth, on grey rainy days and during the long, dark nights, when he was on guard duty—in Poland perhaps, and in Romania. You went with the grunt, who was still enveloped in you, to roll call, and you marched with him in rank and file with a thousand other coats past His Majesty, who was pleased to see how many coats his army had. He didn't see the man . . . You were brushed and pounded, and accompanied in your campaigns, appendage-like, by a small, hapless human being, who yearned so for home and quiet, and finally, finally, wanted to sit again with his mother. Mr. Coat, what was enveloped in you was not lazy or lethargic, and the front also did not stab him in the back. He was just a man . . .

You had it good, dear coat. You felt nothing, and in this way you were, to a certain degree, a soldier's ideal. And at the end of the day, when we think properly, the coat mattered a great deal more than what lay inside it. Inside the room, you, the coat, were pampered, counted, and guarded carefully. The men were cheap, as cheap as

schen waren billig, billig wie die hingeschlachteten Jungen von Langemarck...

Lieber alter Mantel! Was hast du schon alles gesehen! Brutalitäten und Not und Hunger und Blut und Todeszuckungen und Offiziere in hellen, bequemen Kraftwagen und Paraden und Lügen, Lügen, Lügen ... Du bist weit in der Welt herumgekommen, und jetzt trägt dich seine Frau oder seine Schwester, und sie versucht, sich in deinem dünnen, fadenscheinig gewordenen Stoff zu wärmen. Kriegsjahre, diese Kriegsjahre zählen siebenfach – schier dreißig Jahre bist du alt. Ruh dich aus, du hast genug erlebt. Hast gesehen, wie ein Volk zugrunde ging, weil vierzehn Millionen Mäntel draußen waren und kein Kopf. Aber wozu braucht der alte Preuße einen Kopf? ...

Leb wohl! lieber alter Mantel.

the men butchered in Langemarck [in the battle of Ypres in Belgium] . . .

Dear old coat! What you have seen! Brutality, distress, and hunger, and blood, and death throes, and officers in bright, comfortable automobiles, and parades, and lies, lies, lies . . . You have travelled widely in the world, and now his wife or sister wears you, trying to warm herself in your thin, threadbare material. The war years, these war years, count seven fold—you are surely thirty years old. Rest, you have experienced enough. You have seen how a nation has perished, because there were fourteen million coats in the field, but no head. But why does an old Prussian need a head? . . .

Fare well, dear old coat.

Kurt Tucholsky

Die Flecke

Ignaz Wrobel, *Berliner Volkszeitung*, 21. Dezember 1919, wieder in: *Mona Lisa*.

In der Dorotheenstraße zu Berlin steht das Gebäude der ehemaligen Kriegsakademie. Unten, in guter Mannshöhe, läuft eine Granitlage um das Haus herum, Platte an Platte.

Diese Platten sehen seltsam aus; sie sind weißlich gefleckt, der braune Granit ist hell an vielen Stellen . . . was mag das sein?

Ist er weißlich gefleckt? Aber er sollte rötlich gefleckt sein. Hier hingen, während der großen Zeit, die deutschen Verlustlisten.

Hier hingen, fast alle Tage gewechselt, die schrecklichen Zettel, die endlosen Listen mit Namen, Namen, Namen . . . Ich besitze die Nr. 1 dieser Dokumente: da sind noch sorgfältig die Truppenteile angegeben, wenig Tote stehen auf der ersten Liste, sie waren sehr kurz, diese Nr. 1. Ich weiß nicht, wie viele dann erschienen sind – aber sie gingen hoch hinauf, bis über die Nummer tausend. Namen an Namen – und jedesmal hieß das, daß ein Menschenleben ausgelöscht war oder ›vermißt‹, für die nächste Zukunft ausgestrichen, oder verstümmelt, leicht oder schwer.

Da hingen sie, da, wo jetzt die weißen Flecke sind. Da hingen sie, und vor ihnen drängten sich die Hunderte schweigender Menschen, die ihr Liebstes draußen hatten und die zitterten, daß sie diesen einzigen Namen unter allen den Tausenden hier läsen. Was kümmerten sie die Müllers und Schulzes und Lehmanns, die hier aushingen! Mochten Tausende und Tausende verrecken – wenn er nur nicht dabei war! Und an dieser Gesinnung ertüchtigte der Krieg.

White Spots

Ignaz Wrobel, *Berliner Volkszeitung,* December 21, 1919, again in: Mona Lisa

On Dorotheenstrasse in Berlin, there's a building that once housed the Prussian War Academy. A strip of granite blocks runs around the base of the building, one after another, about as tall as a man.

There's something strange about those blocks; the brown granite looks lighter in many places, as if smudged with white. . . What could this be?

Are they whitish spots? If they're spots, they should be reddish. During the Great War, the lists of German casualties were posted there.

They hung there, changed almost daily, those terrible pages, endless lists with name after name after name. . . I have the very first one of those documents; the military units were still carefully noted on it; that first one listed very few dead; it's very short, list No. 1. I don't know how many appeared after that—just that there were a great many, over a thousand. One name after another, each one signifying a human life snuffed out, or someone "missing"—crossed out for the time being—or injured, or gravely maimed.

There they hung, where the white spots are now. There they hung, and hundreds of people crowded silently around them, people whose loved ones were out there somewhere, trembling, afraid to see that one name among the many thousands. What did they care about the Müllers or Schulzes or Lehmanns posted there! Let them perish, one thousand after another—if only his name doesn't appear! The war thrived on that attitude.

Und an dieser Gesinnung hat es gelegen, daß es vier lange Jahre so gehen konnte. Wären wir alle für einen aufgestanden, alle wie ein Mann –: wer weiß, ob es so lange gedauert hätte. Man hat mir gesagt, ich wisse nicht, wie der deutsche Mann sterben könne. Ich weiß es wohl. Ich weiß aber auch, wie die deutsche Frau weinen kann – und ich weiß, wie sie heute weint, da sie langsam, qualvoll langsam erkennt, wofür er gestorben ist. Wofür . . .

Streue ich Salz in Wunden: Aber ich möchte das himmlische Feuer in Wunden brennen, ich möchte den Trauernden zurufen: Für nichts ist er gestorben, für einen Wahnsinn, für nichts, für nichts, für nichts.

Im Laufe der Jahre werden ja diese weißen Flecke allmählich vom Regen abgewaschen werden und schwinden. Aber diese andern da, die kann man nicht tilgen. In unsern Herzen sind Spuren eingekratzt, die nicht vergehen. Und jedesmal, wenn ich an der Kriegsakademie mit ihrem braunen Granit und den weißen Flecken vorbeikomme, sage ich mir im stillen: Versprich es dir. Lege ein Gelöbnis ab. Wirke. Arbeite. Sags den Leuten. Befreie sie von dem Nationalwahn, du mit deinen kleinen Kräften. Du bist es den Toten schuldig. Die Flecke schreien. Hörst du sie?

Sie rufen: Nie wieder Krieg –!

And it was because of that very attitude that the war could go on like that for four long years. If we had all stood up as one man—who knows if it would have lasted so long. Someone once told me that I didn't know how a German man could die. I know very well how. But I also know how a German woman can cry—and I know she's still crying today, because slowly, excruciatingly slowly, she's beginning to understand what it was that he died for. For what. . . ?

Am I rubbing salt in old wounds? I'd rather burn holy fire in those wounds; I'd like to shout at those who are grieving: He died for nothing, for sheer madness, for nothing. . . for nothing. . . for nothing.

As the years pass by, the rain will gradually wash over those white spots, until they disappear. But there are others that can't be erased. Engraved in our hearts are vestiges that will not fade. And every time I pass by the War Academy, with its brown granite and white spots, I say silently: Promise yourself. Take a vow. Take action. Get to work. Tell people. Liberate them from this national delusion, you, with your modest strengths. You owe it to the dead. Those white spots are screaming. Can you hear them?

They're shouting, "No more war!"

Translated by Cindy Opitz

Kurt Tucholsky

Gebet nach dem Schlachten

Theobald Tiger, *Die Weltbühne,* 7. August 1924, wieder in: *Mit 5 PS*

Kopf ab zum Gebet!
Herrgott! Wir alten vermoderten Knochen
Sind aus den Kalkgräbern noch einmal hervorgekrochen.
Wir treten zum Beten vor dich und bleiben nicht stumm.
Und fragen dich, Gott

Warum?

Warum haben wir unser rotes Herzblut dahingegeben?
Bei unserm Kaiser blieben alle sechs am Leben.
Wir haben einmal geglaubt ... Wir waren schön dumm ...!
Uns haben sie besoffen gemacht ...

Warum?

Einer hat noch sechs Monate im Lazarett geschrien.
Erst das Dörrgemüse und zwei Stabsärzte erledigten ihn.
Einer wurde blind und nahm heimlich Opium.
Drei von uns haben zusammen nur einen Arm ...

Warum – ?

Wir haben Glauben, Krieg, Leben und Alles verloren.
Uns trieben sie hinein wie im Kino die Gladiatoren.
Wir hatten das allerbeste Publikum.
Das starb aber nicht mit ...

Warum –? Warum –?

Prayer After The Slaughter

Theobald Tiger, *Die Weltbühne*, August 7, 1924, again in: *Mit 5 PS*

Heads off for prayer!
Lord God! We old, decaying skeletons
Have crawled once more from our chalky graves.
We now stand before you and will have ourselves heard
as we pray.
And we ask you, Oh God:

Why?

For what did we give the red blood from our hearts away?
The Kaiser has six and they're all still living today.
There was a time we believed ... Oh how stupid we were ...!
They made us all drunk ....

Why?

One of us screamed a full six months in a field hospital bed
Before the dried food and staff doctors finished him off.
Another went blind and hid a stash of opium.
Three of us have but one arm to share among us ...

Why—?

We've all lost our faith, life, the war and whatever we had.
They just threw us in as if we were film gladiators.
We had the best audience you could wish for.
Only it didn't die with us ...

Why?—? Why—?

Herrgott! Herrgott!
Wenn du wirklich Der bist, als den wir dich lernten:
Steig herunter von deinem Himmel, dem besternten!
Fahr hernieder oder schick deinen Sohn!
Reiß ab die Fahnen, die Helme, die Ordensdekoration!
Verkünde den Staaten der Erde, wie wir gelitten,
wie uns Hunger, Läuse, Schrapells und Lügen den Leib zerschnitten!
Feldprediger haben uns in deinem Namen zu Grabe getragen.
Erkläre, daß sie gelogen haben! Läßt du dir das sagen?
Jag uns zurück in unsre Gräber, aber antworte zuvor!
Soweit wir das noch können, knien wir vor dir –
aber leih uns dein Ohr!
Wenn unser Sterben nicht völlig sinnlos war,
verhüte wie 1914 ein Jahr!
Sag es den Menschen! Treib sie zur Desertion!

Wir stehen vor dir: ein Totenbatallion.
Dies blieb uns: zu dir kommen und beten.

Weggetreten!

Prayer After the Slaughter

Lord God! Lord God!
If you're really the one that they taught us about,
Come on down to earth from your heaven with all its stars!
Come on down or at least send us your son!
Tear down the banners, the helmets, the medals for valor!
Announce to the countries of earth how we have suffered;
How hunger, lice, shrapnel and lies left our bodies all broken!
The chaplains have carried every last one of us to our grave in your name.
Declare they have lied! Do we have you to blame?
Chase us back to our graves, but first answer us clear!
As far as we are able, we fall to our knees—
but do lend us your ear!
So that all our dying wasn't just in vain,
Spare us, please, a year like 1914!
Tell all the people! Force them all to desert!

We stand before you, a battalion now dead.
So we come in prayer: all else has been said.

Dismissed!

Berlinica presents

2010–2017 Program

Welcome to Berlinica, the first American publishing company devoted to Berlin! Subscribe to our monthly newsletter at www.berlinica.com, and get a free ebook.

New in 2017:

Kurt Tucholsky

GERMANY? GERMANY!
SATIRICAL WRITINGS
TRANSLATED BY HARRY ZOHN
Preface by Ralph Blumenthal

Softcover, 200 pp., 5 pictures, $14.95
ISBN: 978-1-935902-38-6

". . . the most brilliant, prolific, and witty cultural journalist of his time"

Cornelia Dömer

MARTIN LUTHER'S TRAVEL GUIDE
500 YEARS OF THE 95 THESES. ON THE TRAIL OF THE REFORMATION IN GERMANY

Softcover, 176pp., full color
120 pictures and 14 maps, $13.95
ISBN: 978-1-935902-44-7

Sebastian Ringel

LEIPZIG!
ONE THOUSAND YEARS OF GERMAN HISTORY
BACH, LUTHER, FAUST: THE CITY OF BOOKS AND MUSIC

Softcover, 224 pp., color, $25.95
ISBN: 978-1-935902-58-1

"Humorous and touching stories from thousand years of Leipzig"

Erik Kirschbaum

BURNING BEETHOVEN
THE ERADICATION OF GERMAN CULTURE IN THE UNITED STATES IN WORLD WAR I
Preface by Herb Stupp

Softcover, 176 pp., 20 pictures, $14.95, ISBN: 978-1-935902-85-0

"Powerful retelling of a forgotten piece of American history"

Andreas Nachama
Julius Schoeps
Hermann Simon

JEWS IN BERLIN

Preface by Carol Kahn-Strauss

Softcover, 314 pp., $25.95
376 pictures, color & b/w
ISBN: 978-1-935902-60-7

"... a captivating read that promises a wealth of enjoyment..."

Monika Maertens

BERLIN FOR FREE

A GUIDEBOOK TO MOVIES, MUSEUMS, MUSIC, AND MORE FOR THE FRUGAL TRAVELER

Softcover, 104 pp., $11.95
ISBN: 978-1-935902-40-9

"This book is an investment that pays for itself—whoever wants, or has to save, needs it"

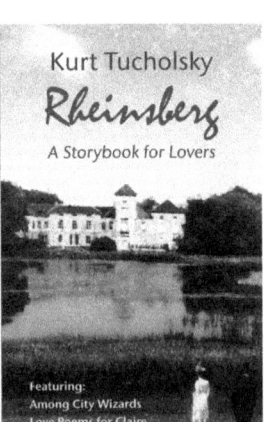

Kurt Tucholsky

RHEINSBERG

A STORYBOOK FOR LOVERS

WITH: AMONG CITY WIZARDS
Afterword by Peter Boethig

Hardcover, 96 pp., 35 pictures, $14.95
ISBN: 978-1-935902-25-6

"This book was the blueprint for love for an entire Generation"

Michael Brettin / Peter Kroh

BERLIN 1945
WORLD WAR II:
PHOTOS OF THE AFTERMATH

From the Soviet Army Archives
With a Preface by Steven Kinzer

Softcover, 218 pp., 177 bw photos
$25.95, ISBN: 978-1-935902-02-7

"Even if you think you've seen it all, Berlin 1945 will surprise you"

Thomas Flemming

BERLIN IN THE COLD WAR–THE BATTLE FOR THE DIVIDED CITY

Softcover, 90 pp., $11.95
51 bw pictures, 3 maps
ISBN: 978-1-935902-80-5

"The story of a divided in a nutshell, without missing a beat"

Michael Cramer

THE BERLIN WALL TODAY

REMNANTS, RUINS REMEMBRANCES

Softcover, 100 pp., $15.95
Full color, 150 pictures,
ISBN: 978-1-935902-10-2

"A well-illustrated book"

Erik Kirschbaum

ROCKING THE WALL

BRUCE SPRINGSTEEN: THE BERLIN CONCERT THAT CHANGED THE WORLD

Softcover, 168 pp., 45 color pictures, $16.95, ISBN: 978-1-935902-82-9

"A statement of the power of music as anyone, ever, has come up with"

Andreas Austilat

MARK TWAIN IN BERLIN

NEWLY DISCOVERED STORIES & AN ACCOUNT OF TWAIN'S BERLIN ADVENTURES
Preface by Lewis Lapham

Softcover, 176 pp., 67 bw pictures, $13.95, ISBN: 978-1-935902-95-9

"This fascinating book is a must-read for any Twain enthusiast"

Holly-Jane Rahlens

WALLFLOWER

A BERLIN NOVEL

Softcover, 146 pp., $12.95
ISBN: 978-1-935902-70-6

". . . an absorbing story of two people who are trying to figure out who they are and a fascinating look at the dawning of a new era in Germany . . ."

Monika Maertens

BERLIN FOR FREE

A GUIDEBOOK TO MOVIES, MUSEUMS, MUSIC, AND MORE FOR THE FRUGAL TRAVELER

Softcover, 104 pp., $11.95
ISBN: 978-1-935902-40-9

"This book is an investment that pays for itself—whoever wants, or has to save, needs it"

Lothar Heinke

WINGS OF DESIRE ANGELS OF BERLIN

Softcover, 102 pp., $19.95
123 full color pictures
ISBN: 978-1-935902-18-8

"A book full of anecdotes about the angels throughout the city – and a search for angelic traces"

Rose Marie Donhauser

THE BERLIN COOKBOOK

TRADITIONAL RECIPES AND NOURISHING STORIES

Hardcover, 104 pp., $21.95
61 recipes, 98 color pictures
ISBN: 978-1-935902-51-5

"Beautiful pictures, entertaining texts, and easy to process, fresh ingredients"

Adrienne Haan

BERLIN – MON AMOUR

A TRIBUTE TO 1920S GERMANY IN MUSIC

Music CD, 50 minutes
In English or German
$ 15.95, only on Amazon

"Grace, elegance, power"

Rosemarie Reed

THE PATH TO NUCLEAR FISSION

NARRATED BY LINDA HUNT

Movie DVD, run time 81 min
German / English, subtitled
$19.95, only on Amazon

"... honors the lives of women who were more than significant ..."

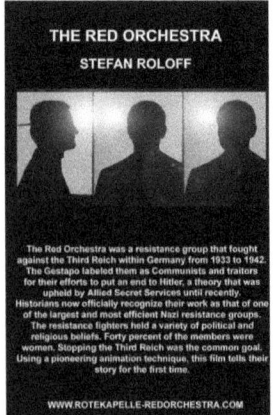

Stefan Roloff

THE RED ORCHESTRA

A DOCUMENTARY ABOUT THE GERMAN ANTI-NAZI RESISTANCE

Movie DVD, run time 57 min.
German and English, subtitled
$24.95, only on Amazon

"... danger invaded normalcy ... landscape threatens to tumble ..."

www.ingramcontent.com/pod-product-compliance
Lightning Source LLC
LaVergne TN
LVHW050141080526
838202LV00062B/6542